Electric Guitars
and Basses

▾ ▾ ▾

A PHOTOGRAPHIC HISTORY

Electric Guitars
and Basses

A PHOTOGRAPHIC HISTORY

▼ ▼ ▼ ▼ ▼

George Gruhn & Walter Carter

GPI Books

An Imprint of

mf Miller Freeman Books

San Francisco

▼ ▼ ▼

GPI Books
An Imprint of Miller Freeman Books
600 Harrison Street, San Francisco, CA 94107

Publishers of *Guitar Player* and
Bass Player Magazines
A member of the United Newspapers Group

Library of Congress Cataloging-in-Publication Data
Gruhn, George.
    Electric guitars and basses : a photographic
history / George Gruhn & Walter Carter.
       p.   cm.
    Includes bibliographical references (p.)
and index.
    ISBN 0-87930-328-X
     1. Guitar—United States—Pictorial works.
I. Carter, Walter. II. Title.
ML1015.G9G763 1994
787.87' 1973—dc20   94-10418

Designed by Brad Greene, Greene Design

Printed in Hong Kong

98 97 96 95 94   5 4 3 2 1

TABLE OF CONTENTS
▼ ▼ ▼

Introduction 1

PART ONE
Electric Roots: 1932 to World War II

Hawaiians

Rickenbacker 8

National 14

Gibson 20

Fender 31

Other makers 35

Spanish-necks

Vivi-Tone 42

Solidbodies 47

Hollowbodies 53

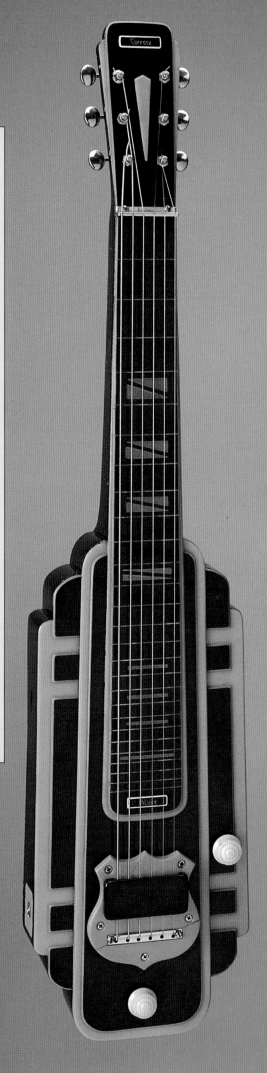

PART TWO
Branches of the Electric Family: 1947 to the 1990s

Full-depth Hollowbodies

Gibson 65

Epiphone 82

Gretsch 89

Other Makers 107

Solidbodies

Fender 115

Fender Basses 133

Fender Colors 139

Gibson 148

Gretsch 171

Rickenbacker 181

Other Makers 186

Thinbodies

Gibson 203

Epiphone 216

Rickenbacker 223

Other Makers 232

Afterword:
The Future of the Guitar 245

Bibliography 248

Index 249

INTRODUCTION

▼ ▼ ▼

Electric guitars have existed side by side with acoustic guitars since the early 1930s, but from an evolutionary point of view, the two barely overlap. All the modern acoustic guitar styles—flat top, archtop, and resonator—were perfected by 1935, the year that major guitar manufacturers such as Gibson, Epiphone, and National brought their first electric models to market. This year provides a convenient line of demarcation for the authors, for this book is not only a focused study of electric instruments but also the second part of a two-volume photographic history of American guitars, banjos, and mandolins.

Although both volumes have a similar appearance, with hundreds of color photographs of interesting and important instruments, the two have some significant differences. This book encompasses about 50 years of fretted instrument evolution, less than half the period covered by the first volume, and it focuses primarily on only one type of instrument. The period from the 1830s to the 1930s, which is the scope of the first volume, began with the guitar, then moved on to the five-string banjo, the mandolin, and the tenor banjo, then finally saw the guitar's ultimate rise to dominant position in the fretted instrument world. This past 50 years, however, begins with and continues with the electric guitar—not electric fretted instruments, just electric guitars. Electric banjos were never more than curiosities; electric mandolins were a bit more successful but still never a threat to acoustic mandolins; and electric Hawaiian guitars, which ushered in the electric era, survive today primarily through their highly specialized, highly mechanized offshoot, the pedal steel.

The electric guitar has struggled, more so than the various acoustic fretted instruments that preceded it, for acceptance as a type of instrument to be judged on its own merits rather than against acoustic guitars. Musicians and music lovers have derided it for not having a true amplified acoustic guitar sound. Designers and craftsmen have dismissed it on the simplistic grounds that little luthiery skill is required to attach a set of electronics to a plank of wood. Consequently, the aesthetic qualities of electric guitars have not always been fully recognized, even though the very nature of the instrument—the secondary importance of acoustic qualities—offers a freedom of design unavailable to designers of acoustic instruments.

The electric guitar has come into its own in the last decade, with its own set of classic designs, legends, and lore. The Fender Stratocaster solidbody and the Gibson ES-335 semi-hollowbody are to the electric guitar world what the Martin dreadnought flat top or the Gibson L-5 archtop are to the acoustic world. The parallel extends to the obscure end of the spectrum: The Coral electric sitar of the late 1960s has much in common with the harp guitar of the early 1900s; not only do they both have an extra set of strings but they were both interesting experiments and commercial failures. To the guitar aficionado nowadays, a prominent tiger-stripe wood grain in the maple top of a 1960 Gibson Les Paul Standard looks as beautiful as a highly figured piece of Brazilian rosewood on a prewar Martin D-45 acoustic flat top, and the curves and contours of a Fender Stratocaster body are as classic as the scroll and *f*-holes of a Gibson F-5 mandolin. The names Adolph Rickenbacker and Leo Fender have become as familiar and revered as C. F. Martin and Orville Gibson.

The instruments alone may deserve a book, but the stories of the major manufacturers—whether they involve revolutionary innovations, utter lack of foresight, or both—have proven irresistible. It seems inconceivable that Gibson would fail to recognize a growing demand in the 1960s for its discontinued Les Paul Standard and, when it finally noticed the demand, would reintroduce a version that was *not the right one*. It seems inexplicable that Fender could come up with the superbly designed Stratocaster and later literally throw together new "models" from surplus parts; though, considering that management had shifted out of the creative hands of the company founder and into the domain of corporate "bean counters," it does seem almost logical. Some of today's most collectible models, such as Gibson's Flying V and Explorer, were dismal commercial failures and are consequently quite rare, while others, like the Fender Stratocaster and the Gibson Les Paul Standard, were successful in 1950s versions and are not rare at all by vintage guitar standards. Yet they still bring premium prices on the vintage market because of the perfection of their design.

In the world of vintage fretted instruments, one story leads to another, and we could go on forever. We have tried to let the photographs do most of the talking, however, and they are offered for your enjoyment and appreciation.

We would like to thank the many collectors and dealers who let us photograph their instruments. We are indebted to the following people for sharing their knowledge in specialized areas: for Vivi-Tone: Roger Siminoff and John Sprung; for early Epiphone and National: Mike Newton; for early Fender: Gary Bohannon and John Sprung.

George Gruhn

Walter Carter

Nashville, 1994

Credits: Ownership credit for instruments refers to the time at which the instrument was photographed. Photographers are identified by their initials. They are: Walter Carter, Dean Dixon, Steve Evans, Dan Loftin, Billy Mitchell, Mike Newton, and John Sprung.

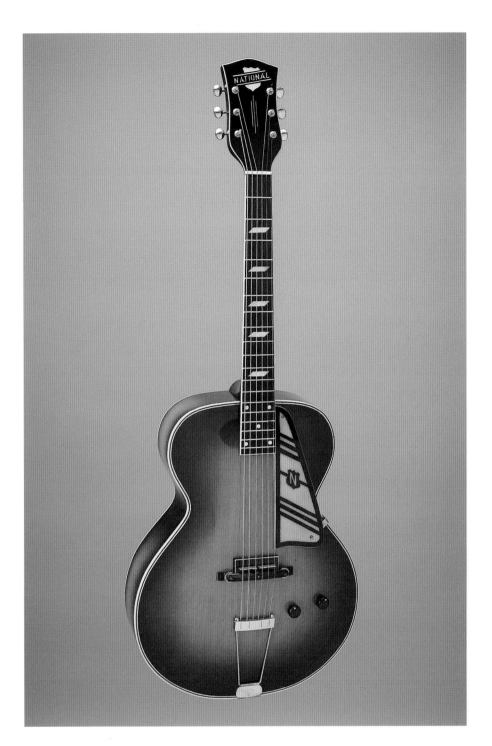

PART ONE

▼ ▼ ▼

Electric Roots:
1932 to World War II

The single most powerful force throughout the evolution of American fretted instruments has been the quest for greater volume. Regardless of the era—acoustic or electric—it is a rare musician who has not sought a louder instrument.

In the 1920s the demand for louder stringed instruments was spurred by the development of phonographs and radio. Commercial AM radio debuted in late 1919, bringing with it a new technology for electrical sound reproduction. In 1925 that technology was incorporated into the production of records, and by the end of the decade phonograph makers had switched to electronic sound amplification. With the public's ear accustomed to louder radios and phonographs, louder instruments could not be far behind. By the early 1930s acoustic instrument designs had been refined and perfected to the point where they had reached their practical and physical limitations, and there was nowhere to go for greater volume except in an altogether new direction—electrical amplification.

Visionaries had begun experimenting with electrified instruments in the 1920s. As early as 1924 Gibson had designs for electric instruments ready to be developed, but management balked at the futuristic idea and three key executives resigned in frustration. The idea proved to be not so futuristic after all. Only four years later, Vega unveiled an electric banjo at a convention of instrument makers. *The Crescendo* magazine described it in the January 1929 issue: "The device consisted of a unit attached to the head of the banjo which transmitted the tone to a portable amplifying unit and radio loudspeaker."

Already there was innovation and competition in the electric field. The article went on to describe a new product from Stromberg-Voisinet: "It can be operated on either AC or DC currents. It consists of an electric pick-up and an amplifier. The pick-up is affixed to the sound board of a guitar or the bridge of a banjo and converts the vibrations into electrical impulses. These are conducted to the amplifier which produces the tone quality required."

Vega's choice of a banjo for its first electric instrument is not surprising in light of the tenor banjo's domination of the fretted instrument market in the 1920s and Vega's position as a leading banjo maker since the early years of the twentieth century. But changes were brewing. A Stromberg-Voisinet ad in 1929 pictured two electric flat top guitars along with two electric banjos. The guitar was indeed poised to take over as the dominant fretted instrument, but the electric guitar that emerged would be an *f*-hole archtop and not an electric flat top.

Vega did become a minor competitor in the electric guitar market by the late 1930s, and Stromberg-Voisinet, after a name change to Kay, would become one of the most successful makers of low-priced instruments. But neither of these early players in the electric field would make a significant mark in the development of electric guitars.

The company that would make history with the first electric guitar utilizing a modern pickup did not even exist in 1929. Ro-Pat-In (later Rickenbacker) was formed in 1932, appropriately enough for the specific purpose of making electric guitars, and it succeeded where others had failed for at least two reasons. The first was the pickup. Earlier pickups were microphonic, depending on a mechanical transfer of vibrations from the strings, through either the air or a wooden bridge. The Ro-Pat-In pickup accomplished the transfer electromagnetically, with the metal strings disturbing a magnetic field to produce electric signals. This more direct magnetic design produced greater volume than the microphonic pickup, but the instrument's natural acoustic tone was sacrificed—a sacrifice that players and audiences would be slow to accept.

The second element of Ro-Pat-In's success was its choice of musicians to target. They were not the banjo players of the early 1930s, who were already playing some of the loudest, most piercing acoustic instruments ever made. Nor were they "Spanish-neck" (standard) guitarists, who in 1932 could choose between resonator models made by National and Dobro, large-bodied *f*-hole archtops from Gibson and Epiphone, and large-bodied flat tops from Martin and Gibson. All of these highly evolved guitars produced much more volume than the typical guitars of the mid-1920s. Moreover, they could equal the volume produced by the early electric guitars and amplifiers, with a decidedly superior tone, especially when played chordally as a rhythm instrument.

Ro-Pat-In made its first guitar for the musicians who most needed extra volume in the early 1930s: Hawaiian guitarists. Even the loudest acoustic guitar lost some of its punch when played in the lap, Hawaiian style. Electrical amplification brought the Hawaiian guitarist up to the volume level of the rest of the band. In addition, the greater sustaining power of a solidbody electric guitar proved to be perfectly suited for Hawaiian music, and it more than offset the loss of acoustic tonal qualities. Consequently, in the electric era prior to World War II, Hawaiian guitars, also known as "steel guitars" and "lap steels," were far more successful commercially than the standard or Spanish-neck electrics.

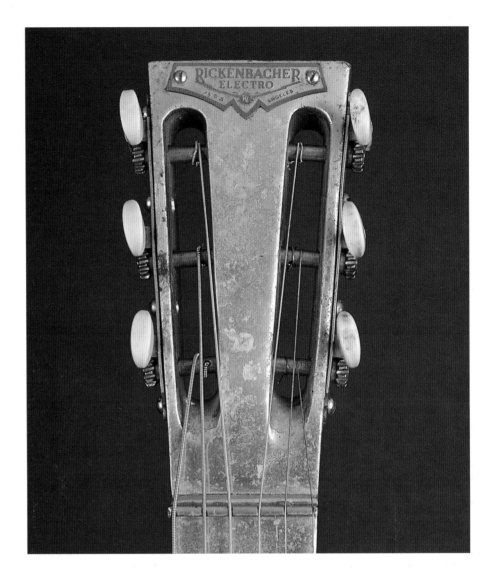

▶ *Rickenbacker A-25, circa 1935. The Frying Pan, Pan-handle, or—Adolph Ricken-backer's favorite name for it—the Pancake is the first production model with a modern magnetic pickup. The 25 in the model name refers to the 25-inch scale. Literature and advertising spelled Rickenbacker with a* k, *but peghead nameplates used the original spelling—Rickenbacher—until the 1950s. The factory installed the tuners to extend from the back of the instrument, but many players turned them over for easier access. Gruhn Guitars/WC*

HAWAIIANS

▼ ▼ ▼

Rickenbacker

One of the most famous names in the history of the electric guitar belonged to a tool and die maker. His involvement in guitar production came not from any musical interest but through his job of supplying metal parts to a guitar manufacturer. Nevertheless, he was in the right place at the right time, and he had the foresight and the production engineering skill to become the first to market a modern electric guitar and the first to build a successful company exclusively around electric instruments.

He was born Adolph Rickenbacher in Switzerland in 1892 and came to the United States as a child. He moved to Los Angeles in 1918 and formed the Rickenbacker Manufacturing Company in 1925, changing the spelling of his

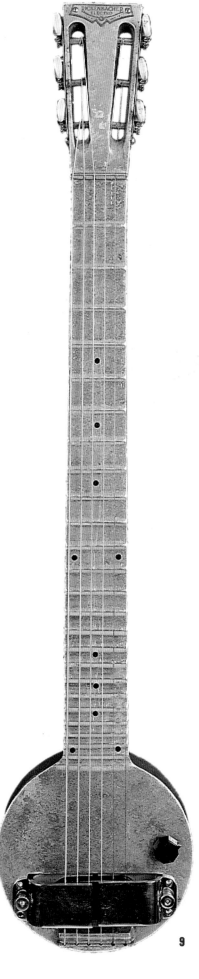

name to take advantage of his distant kinship with World War I flying ace Eddie Rickenbacker. It was Rickenbacker's shop that the National company hired to make metal bodies for resonator guitars. When National's innovative models succeeded, the company not only located a new factory near Rickenbacker's shop but also bought new equipment for him. In 1928 Rickenbacker bought 13 shares of National stock and was given the title (in catalogs if not officially) of company engineer.

National's principals were constantly fighting in the early years of the company. Disagreements over the electric guitar prompted George Beauchamp, a founding partner and general manager, Rickenbacker, and others to form the Ro-Pat-In Corporation (the significance of the name is unknown) on October 15, 1931. They set up shop next to Rickenbacker's tool and die. Less than a month later, Beauchamp was ousted by National's board.

Beauchamp had been experimenting with electric pickup designs, and he settled on a pair of horseshoe-shaped magnets surrounding a coil of wire, which itself surrounded six individual magnets (one for each string on the guitar). In concept, it was the modern electric guitar pickup. Beauchamp had been a Hawaiian-style guitarist on the vaudeville circuit, and National's first models had been squareneck Hawaiians, so it is not surprising that his patent application drawing and the actual prototype instrument were Hawaiian guitars.

▲ *Century Singing Electric, mid-1930s. The nameplate reads "Century Singing Electric" but the horseshoe pickup is that of a Rickenbacker. Rickenbacker did not make its own aluminum bodies, and whether it finished out the guitar for another distributor or simply supplied the pickup is unknown. Mike Cass/WC*

The prototype was made of wood, but the production model, introduced in mid-1932, was cast aluminum—made not by Rickenbacker but by the Aluminum Alloy Casting Company. The guitar sounded different from any previous instrument, and it looked different too, with a small, circular body that inspired the nickname "Frying Pan." A grand total of 13 Frying Pans were sold in 1932. Ro-Pat-In also introduced a Spanish-neck, *f*-hole archtop model with a wood body supplied by the Harmony company of Chicago, and four of these models were sold in 1932.

The company's slow start was made all the more frustrating by the United States Patent Office's delays. Beauchamp filed on June 8, 1932, but the patent was not granted until August 10, 1937. By that time the market was flooded with instruments employing his pickup design. A legal battle would have been costly, but Beauchamp could take some consolation in the fact that the electric Hawaiian guitar had become popular and that his company was the leading maker of the new instruments.

Ro-Pat-In's first instruments bore the Electro brand. In 1934 the company name was changed to the Electro String Instrument Corporation and the instruments marketed as Rickenbacker Electro models. Nameplates on instruments, however, said "Rickenbacher" with an *h* until the 1950s. The reason for the inconsistency is unknown and may possibly be something as simple as a mistake on the part of the nameplate supplier.

Prior to World War II, lap steels were far more important to Rickenbacker's success than were Spanish electrics. After a hiatus from July 1942 to early 1946, when Rickenbacker (like most guitar makers) diverted its effort to war products, the company continued to focus on lap steels. In December 1953 Adolph Rickenbacker sold the company to F. C. Hall, founder of the Radio-Tel electronics company, an early distributor for Fender products. Appropriately, the company that established the market for electric guitars would continue to make electric instruments exclusively (except for a handful of custom-made acoustics in the 1950s and 1960s). Steels played an important part in Rickenbacker's success through the 1950s, thanks in part to an endorsement from musician Jerry Byrd. However, a new line of solidbody guitars introduced in 1954 signaled not only an impending change in the public's taste but a new era for Rickenbacker. By the mid-1960s, Rickenbacker was best known for its sleek, modern thinbodied guitars, and the last Rickenbacker steel guitars were made in 1970.

▼ *Rickenbacker A-22 and amplifier, circa 1935. A Frying Pan with a 22 ½-inch scale, the A-22, appeared soon after the A-25. The cast aluminum body sports a gold look, the result of a lacquer wash. By 1935 Rickenbacker offered six models with the horseshoe pickup: two lap steels, two guitars, a tenor guitar, and a mandolin. However, as the catalog explains, "One style speaker [amplifier] is used for all instruments." Gruhn Guitars/WC*

▼ Rickenbacker B, late 1930s. The heat generated by stage lights or a player's body caused the aluminum Frying Pans to go out of tune, and Rickenbacker tried to solve the problem in 1935 with a Bakelite body. To reduce the weight (bowling balls are made of Bakelite), portions of the body were hollowed out and covered with decorative plates. The plates are chrome-plated on early examples and white-painted on later ones. Prewar Bakelite steels are considered by many Hawaiian players and by rock musician David Lindley, the most visible lap steel player of the 1980s, to be the best instruments of their type ever made. John Sprung/JS

▶ Rickenbacker DC-16, circa 1950. By the time the first electric lap steels appeared, Hawaiian players were experimenting with different tunings. Manufacturers offered guitars with seven, eight, or more strings to provide more harmonic possibilities. Doubleneck models doubled the choices available to a player. This example combines a hollow metal body with Bakelite necks; others have a body and neck of one-piece, hollow metal construction. Postwar horseshoe pickups are narrower than those made in the prewar period. Montana Al/BM

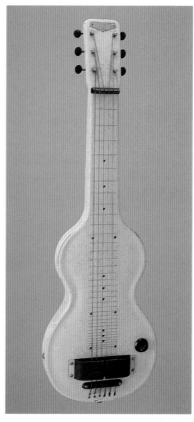

◀ Rickenbacker No. 100, circa 1938 (left). Rickenbacker's new "Silver Hawaiian" lap steel of 1937 brings to mind the nickel-plated resonator guitars made by National—the company that spawned Rickenbacker—in the late 1920s and early 1930s. The chrome-plated brass body is hollow. Gruhn Guitars/DL

◀ Rickenbacker No. 59, circa 1938 (right). This low-end model, introduced in late 1937, has a body stamped out of sheet metal and a crinkled paint finish. It is the predecessor of the popular postwar budget model, the NS or New Style, which is identifiable by a shaded gray finish. Thoroughbred Guitars/BM

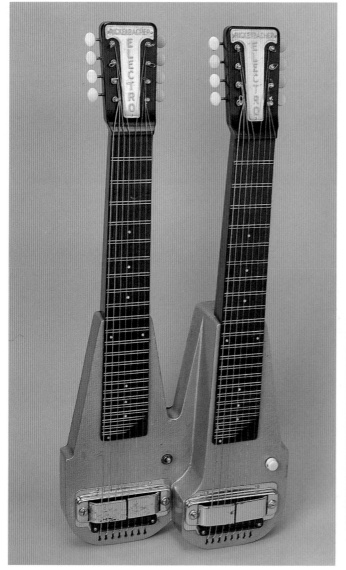

◀ Rickenbacker G, early 1950s. The post–World War II successor to the Silver Hawaiian is the dazzling chrome-and-gold Model G. In 1950 Model G was the most expensive instrument available from Rickenbacker, listing for $292. The DC-16 doubleneck steel was next at $200. The company's best amplifier was $115, and the only Spanish-style guitar model available that year listed for $105. Island Guitars/BM

▶ *National, Supro, and Dobro electric Hawaiians, circa 1935. The first National and Dobro lap steels, like the Rickenbacker Frying Pan, have a cast aluminum body. In contrast to the plain, one-piece look of the Frying Pan, however, these have decorative recessed areas in the top, a wood fingerboard, and an asymmetrical peghead. The Supro kicked off National-Dobro's budget line in 1935, and it does resemble Rickenbacker's Frying Pan. All three models were in production for only about two years before Valco abandoned metal bodies for wood and went on to greater aesthetic expression with such materials as bright paint, pearloid, and clear plastic. Walter Carter/WC*

HAWAIIANS

▼ ▼ ▼

National

National was the first major company to shift its focus from acoustic to electric instruments, a supreme irony in light of the fact that National's refusal to pursue the development of electric guitars in 1931 sparked the formation of Rickenbacker.

National's initial failure to foresee the coming of the electric guitar is even more surprising considering the company's history of innovation. It was incorporated in 1928 in Los Angeles to make and sell the resonator guitars invented by John Dopyera and George Beauchamp. The loudest guitars of their time, the resonators were radically different in construction from conventional guitars, with metal bodies and metal resonator cones. Perhaps the problem in 1931 was a personal one with George Beauchamp rather than a general fear of electric instruments, because National wasted little time after Beauchamp's departure in mounting a serious challenge to Rickenbacker. And when National finally did enter the electric market, the company seemed to be its old fearless self, coming up with new concepts of guitar design from the soundhole-less electric archtops of the late 1930s to the map-shaped, fiberglass-body models of the 1960s.

National cofounder John Dopyera had left in 1928 and formed the Dobro company, but he returned with the merger of National and Dobro in 1932, the same year Rickenbacker introduced the Frying Pan. In 1933 National-Dobro introduced its first electric instrument: a Dobro-brand Spanish-neck guitar. It was not accepted by the playing public, and only a few were made. By 1935, however, Rickenbacker had developed a strong enough market for electric Hawaiian guitars that National-Dobro jumped back in with both feet—actually, to be accurate, with all *three* feet. Electric lap steels, guitars, and mandolins were introduced under three different brands: National, Dobro, and Supro, the latter a newly created budget brand devoted almost exclusively to electric guitars.

By the early 1940s National-Dobro had relocated to Chicago, reorganized under the name Valco, and dropped the Dobro brand, which was eventually reacquired by members of the Dopyera family and is found today on instruments made by the Original Musical Instrument Company. National and Supro were among the more successful lap steel brands well into the 1950s, and Valco continued to make steel guitars until the company's demise in 1968.

▲ *National Silvo, circa 1938. The Silvo, introduced in 1938, combines the metal-body Hawaiian guitar style that brought National into prominence in the late 1920s with the new electric technology. The body is hollow and shaped like a guitar, but the 23-inch scale shows that it is indeed a lap steel. The Silvo electronics unit—the black "ebonoid" disc with pickup and controls—was available as an electric conversion kit for any of National's single-cone resonator models, such as the Duolian, Triolian, or Style O. Dennis Watkins/BM*

▲ National Console, circa 1939. National's first double-neck steel guitar, introduced in 1939, was modeled after the singleneck New Yorker. After World War II the dou-bleneck was given a loftier name—Grand Console—and a cream-and-bronze color scheme. June Dowling/BM

▼ National New Yorker, circa 1942. National was known for eye-catching acoustic resonator guitars with engraved floral designs and etched or painted tropical scenes, and the company's penchant for imaginative ornamentation found a new medium with lap steels. The New Yorker, introduced in 1935, has an art deco look with a shape inspired by the Empire State Building. Early examples have three pickups, two of them concealed beneath the fingerboard. The "tone" selector on the three-pickup model is actually a three-way pickup selector switch. By the time of this example, the New Yorker has a single pickup and a potentiometer for tone control. One of National's more popular models, the New Yorker lasted as long as the company did. Walter Carter/WC

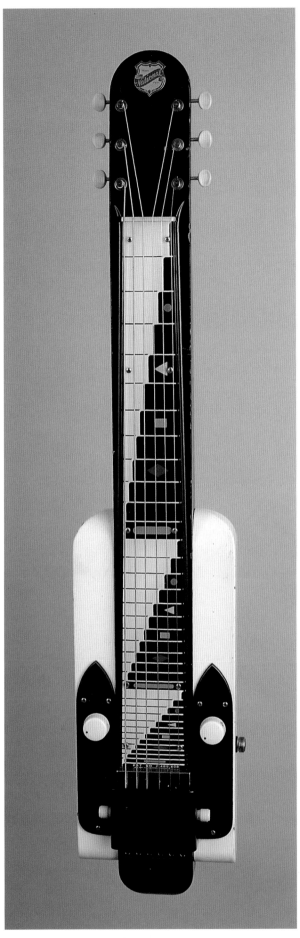

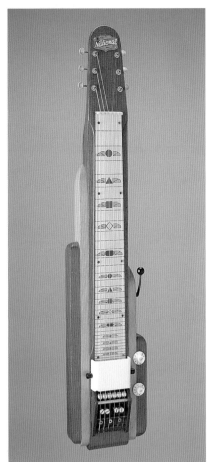

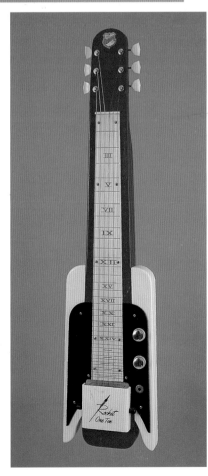

◀ National Dynamic, 1951 (left). The Dynamic added another bold design to the National lineup in 1942. The original version has an asymmetrical stairstep body. This postwar version retains the stairstep motif on the fingerboard, but the body has changed to a symmetrical winged shape. Gruhn Guitars/WC

◀ National Tri-Plex Chord Changer, 1950 (right). National entered the pedal steel market in 1948 with the short-lived Electra-Chord, a two-pedal experiment that looked as much like an exercise bike as a musical instrument. In 1949 the company took a simpler approach to meet the growing demand for pitch-changing devices with the Tri-Plex Chord Changer. A system of cams operated by a lever allows instant switching among three different preset tunings. Kyle Miller/BM

◀ National Rocket 110, 1956. In 1956 National ushered in the Space Age with this rocket-shaped lap steel. Valco made a similar model with black finish for the Gretsch line, where it was called the Jet Airliner. The Rocket 110 lasted only through 1957. Walter Carter/WC

▶ *Supro lap steel, 1955. Pearloid was a popular decorative material in the 1950s, and several models in the Supro line wore a pearloid covering. The strings-through-pickup style is standard on Supro models but found only on a few Nationals of the 1940s. The coil wound around a cardboard bobbin is Valco's cheapest pickup design, but its "dirty" or "screaming" sound has made it popular today— thanks in part to recording artist Ry Cooder, who has mounted a Supro pickup on a standard guitar, and dobroist Jerry Douglas, who often uses an obscure National lap steel with the Supro-style pickup. Gruhn Guitars/WC*

▶ *Coppock Deluxe, mid 1950s (far right). The brand is obscure but the maker (or at least the inspiration) is clear. The elongated peghead ornament graces National's New Yorker and Dynamic models from 1956 onward, and the shield around the pickup is the background shape for National's logo throughout the company's history. The knobs are borrowed from a Rickenbacker lap steel. The palm tree and tropical lagoon (near right) resemble those etched on the back of National's Style O metalbody model of the 1930s. Gordon Dow/BM*

▼ Bronson lap steel and amplifier, mid 1950s. The Bronson company was an instrument distributor that also sold instruments under its own brand. The most common Bronson lap steels were made by Rickenbacker, but this one and its matching amp were clearly made by Valco. John Sprung/JS

19

▶ *Gibson metalbody, 1935. Like Rickenbacker's Frying Pan, Gibson's first electric guitar has a cast aluminum body, but with the double-bout shape of a guitar rather than the Frying Pan's circular form. Following its introduction on October 1, 1935, Gibson salesmen in the field reported that customers thought the metal body did not have the look of quality craftsmanship associated with Gibson. A woodbody version was quickly introduced, and production on the aluminum model ceased on March 9, 1936, after total production of 98. John Sprung/JS*

HAWAIIANS
▾ ▾ ▾

Gibson

The waves of change emanating in late 1932 from a small tool and die shop in Los Angeles did not cause a ripple of concern at the Gibson factory in Kalamazoo, Michigan. Although Gibson had a reputation as a daring, innovative company—having been founded in late 1902 to exploit not just one but two radically new carved-top mandolin and guitar designs—the company had lagged behind other makers in the 1920s when public taste shifted from the mandolin to the tenor banjo. At the end of the decade, however, the guitar overtook the banjo as the dominant fretted instrument, and Gibson's archtop guitars led the company back to the top.

The top position attracted challengers, and in 1932 Gibson was preparing to fight off an onslaught of archtop makers led by Epiphone, one of the more highly respected tenor banjo makers. In addition, the venerable Martin company had just put its large-bodied "dreadnought" flat tops into production, and their success would soon draw Gibson's attention to the flat top market as well. By 1934 Gibson was engaged in fierce competition on two acoustic fronts, counterattacking with larger archtops and a dreadnought-size flat top.

In an arena with such powers as Gibson, Epiphone, and Martin, an upstart company like Rickenbacker could easily go unnoticed. After all, Rickenbacker sold only 28 sets (guitar and amplifier) in 1932, 95 in 1933, and 275 in 1934. That amount barely qualified as a market for electric instruments. Even if sales continued to triple every year—and there was no guarantee that they would—Gibson should have had a grace period of several years before having to contend with the electric guitar.

Furthermore, Gibson general manager Guy Hart was no doubt gun-shy of electric instruments, remembering the upheaval of a decade earlier when the general manager, sales manager, and Gibson's legendary quality control supervisor, Lloyd Loar, had all resigned in a dispute over electrics. In 1933 Loar and his associates had formed the Vivi-Tone company to market new concepts for electric and acoustic instruments, and Hart would likely have monitored the electric guitar market by watching Vivi-Tone, which was based in Kalamazoo, rather than the California-based Rickenbacker company. Hart must have felt quite secure when Vivi-Tone forsook guitars for keyboards by 1934.

In 1935, however, Rickenbacker sales made a significant jump to 1,288 sets, a signal that guitar players were accepting the new electrics. Gibson read the sign and introduced its first electric model, a metalbody lap steel, in October 1935. A woodbody model replaced it at the beginning of 1936. A second lap steel model and the company's first electric hollowbody guitar followed later in 1936, and by the end of the year Gibson was committed to the electric guitar.

As it had in the banjo market of the 1920s, Gibson made up for a late start with a flurry of innovation. Catalogs, usually published every two years,

could not keep up with new pickups and new models in the late 1930s and early 1940s. World War II put electric guitar evolution on hold, but Gibson picked up after the war with more new designs, some for standard guitars as well as lap steels.

Like most companies, Gibson recognized the severe decline of interest in Hawaiian guitars by the late 1950s.—a decline hastened by the rising popularity of the pedal steel. Gibson offered several pedal steel models, but its postwar pitch-changing mechanism was not as advanced as that of some other makers. Except for one year, 1949, annual pedal steel sales never reached 100 instruments, and the last were made in 1966. By 1960 the lap steel line was down to two models, and the last lap steels were made in 1967.

◀ *Gibson EH-150, 1939. The EH-150 was introduced on January 1, 1936, to replace Gibson's original metalbody model. "EH" stands for Electric Hawaiian; "150" is the price of the instrument with amplifier. The maple body and rich sunburst finish gave this instrument the "Gibson look" that customers wanted. A cheaper woodbody model with black paint finish, the EH-100, was also introduced in 1936 at a list price (with companion amplifier) of $100. Gruhn Guitars/DL*

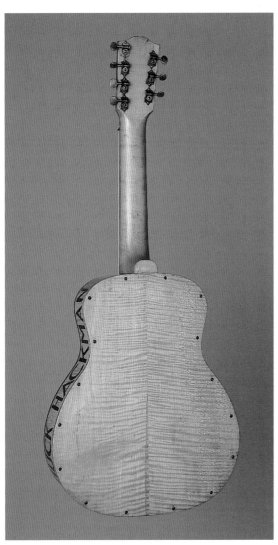

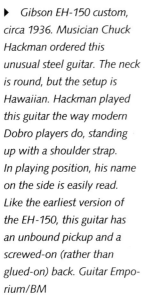

▶ *Gibson EH-150 custom, circa 1936. Musician Chuck Hackman ordered this unusual steel guitar. The neck is round, but the setup is Hawaiian. Hackman played this guitar the way modern Dobro players do, standing up with a shoulder strap. In playing position, his name on the side is easily read. Like the earliest version of the EH-150, this guitar has an unbound pickup and a screwed-on (rather than glued-on) back. Guitar Emporium/BM*

23

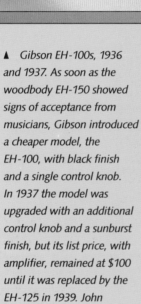

▲ Gibson EH-100s, 1936 and 1937. As soon as the woodbody EH-150 showed signs of acceptance from musicians, Gibson introduced a cheaper model, the EH-100, with black finish and a single control knob. In 1937 the model was upgraded with an additional control knob and a sunburst finish, but its list price, with amplifier, remained at $100 until it was replaced by the EH-125 in 1939. John Sprung/JS

▶ Gibson EH-150 custom 13-string, circa 1937. Most makers of Hawaiian electrics offered 6-, 7-, or 8-string models, and musician Eddie Alkire was playing a 10-string lap steel by the early 1940s. This 13-string single-neck is most unusual. Brattle Guitars/BM

◄ *Gibson Doubleneck Electric Hawaiian, 1937. Most players felt that a doubleneck lap steel provided a more practical solution to the need for greater harmonic variety than a single-neck guitar with 10 or more strings. Consequently, Gibson introduced this doubleneck version of the EH-150 in 1937. The body size of a doubleneck makes it unwieldy in a player's lap, however, and Gibson replaced it with a "console" model—with legs—in 1939. Gruhn Guitars/WC*

▼ *Recording King Roy Smeck AB-104, 1938. Electric guitars were beginning to catch on by 1938, as shown by the appearance of an endorsement model. Roy Smeck, the vaudeville star known as the Wizard of the Strings, endorsed more models than any other recording star; he already had two acoustic Hawaiians in the Gibson line. This Smeck lap steel was made by Gibson for sale under Montgomery Ward's house brand. Gruhn Guitars/DL*

▼ *Gibson EH-185s and EH-185 amplifier, 1940. Despite the commercial failure of the original metalbody model, Gibson did not give up on metal as a material for lap steels. The EH-185 debuted in 1939 with a single metal piece that starts as the mounting plate for the pickup and controls, then extends under the fingerboard to end up as the peghead. The hexagonal pickup was replaced by the oval style, with height-adjustable pole pieces, in 1940. The companion amplifier features a control assembly that can be lifted out of the speaker cabinet. Walter Carter/WC*

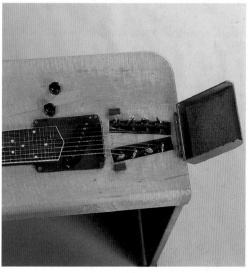

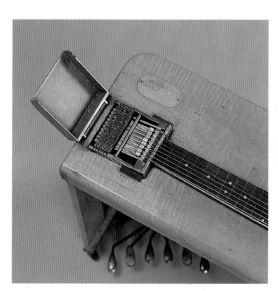

◀ *Gibson Electraharp, 1939. To play the sophisticated music of late 1930s dance bands, steel guitarists developed different tunings, but retuning between songs posed an obvious problem. Machinist John Moore and noted musician Alvino Rey developed for Gibson this electric pedal model, which features a modern "double-fingered" mechanism capable of raising or lowering each individual string pitch. The workings of the instrument are hidden behind an attractive maple and walnut cabinet with wooden covers for the pitch-changers and tuners. Unfortunately for Gibson, the Harlin Brothers of Indianapolis had already patented a similar design for their Multi-Kord pedal steels and sued for infringement. Gibson's postwar pedal models used a different type of mechanism. Gibson product demonstrator Wilbur Marker told the* Kalamazoo Gazette *in 1941 that 35 Electraharps had been made, but Gibson records show only 13 instruments shipped. Gruhn Guitars/DL*

► *Gibson EH-630, 1960. Gibson's postwar Electraharp does not measure up to the prewar version aesthetically or functionally. With this more primitive pitch-changing system, the pitch of an individual string can be lowered only by lowering all the strings and then raising all but one back to original pitch. To its credit, the Electraharp was fitted with a double-coil humbucking pickup in 1956, a year before humbuckers appeared on standard Gibson guitars. Gruhn Guitars/WC*

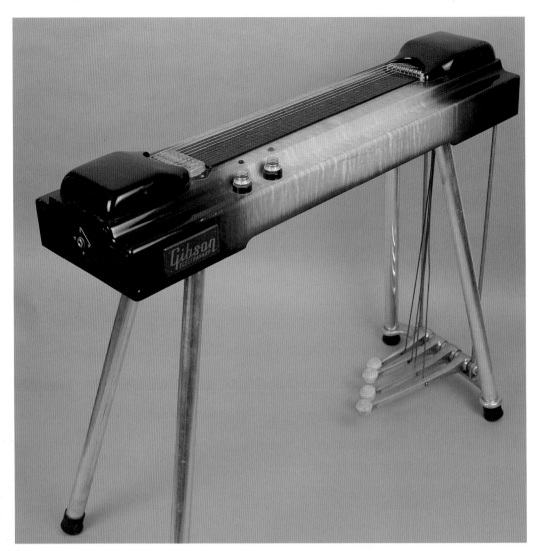

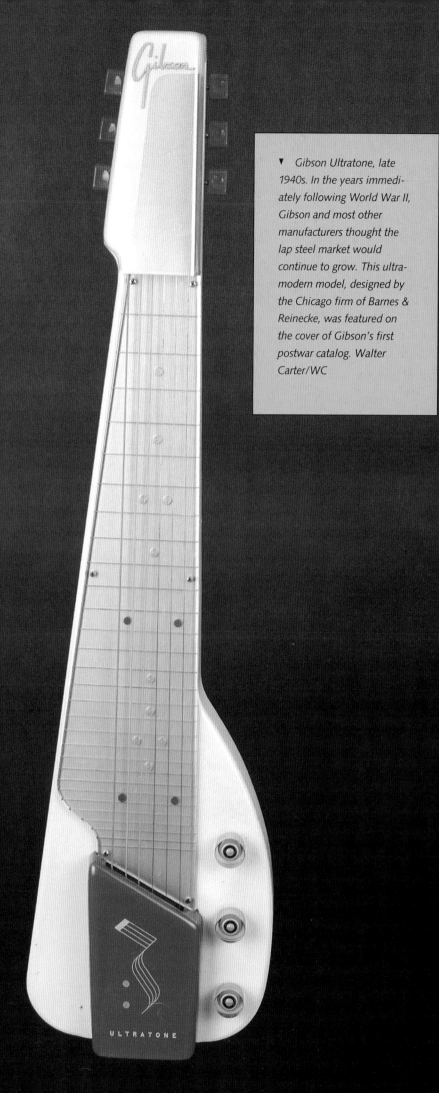

▼ Gibson Ultratone, late 1940s. In the years immediately following World War II, Gibson and most other manufacturers thought the lap steel market would continue to grow. This ultra-modern model, designed by the Chicago firm of Barnes & Reinecke, was featured on the cover of Gibson's first postwar catalog. Walter Carter/WC

▶ *Gibson Ultratone, mid 1950s. Ultratones are among the most colorful instruments ever made by Gibson. Finishes include deep blue, salmon, black, brown, and this ivory-and-mahogany combination. The top aged to a golden hue makes this lap steel resemble Gibson's gold-top solidbody electric guitar, the Les Paul. Walter Carter/WC*

▶ *Gibson Skylark, 1958 (far right). As the Consolette was going out of production, Gibson introduced a singleneck korina lap steel. The Skylark is noteworthy because of its association with the two Gibson guitars most highly valued by collectors: the korina-body Flying V and Explorer of 1958. Unlike the korina guitars, however, the Skylark was a budget model that was by far Gibson's most successful lap steel during its production period of 1956 through 1967. Kyle Miller/BM*

▼ *Gibson Consolette, late 1950s. The Consolette, a doubleneck with legs, debuted in 1952. In keeping with Gibson's flashy new designs, it featured a new type of wood—African limba or, as Gibson would later call it, "korina" wood. Catalogs of the period describe it simply as "mahogany type." The model was last made in 1956, but korina wood would go on to greater fame with the Explorer and Flying V guitars. Jay Levin/BM*

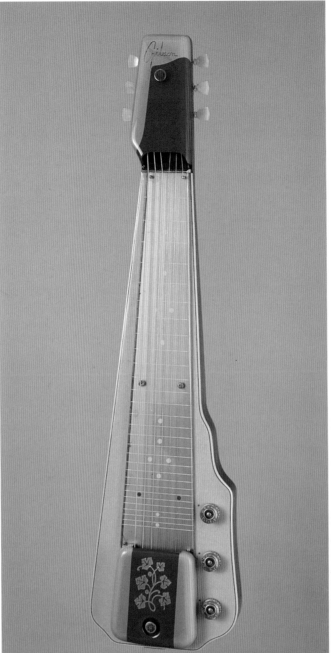

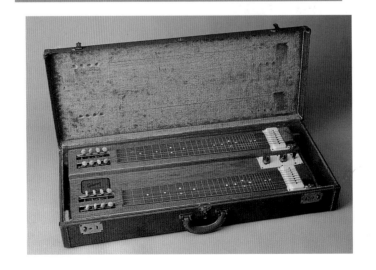

HAWAIIANS

▼ ▼ ▼

Fender

Late in 1945, while all the major guitar manufacturers were gearing up for an expected postwar boom, a couple of tinkerers got together in Fullerton, California. Clayton Orr (Doc) Kauffman was a guitarist and the inventor of the side-pull vibrato unit found on some prewar Rickenbacker and Gibson electric guitars. Clarence Leo Fender, owner of a radio repair business, had never learned how to tune—much less play—a guitar, but his interest in electronics had led him to build a rather primitive solidbody electric guitar in 1943.

Kauffman and Fender formed the K&F company and began making lap steels and amplifiers. From the look of their products, K&F would seem doomed to failure. The metal logo plate sported a lightning bolt, but that was the flashiest feature of a K&F lap steel. Its pinewood body was shaped like a short oar, and the finish was battleship gray, black, or natural, with stenciled fingerboard markers. The earliest examples, according to legend, were baked in the kitchen oven in Fender's home. These Plain Janes had to compete with Rickenbacker's eye-catching black-and-white Bakelite model, Gibson's modernistic bodies, and National's colorful art deco ornamentation.

The K&F pickup was unique in that the coil—the windings of wire— encircled the strings rather than a magnet or magnets. It achieved what was probably the most direct link from string to electronic signal, but it was not very powerful. K&F amps, too, were small and plain, not nearly as pretty or as powerful as those of any major manufacturer.

Among those with little faith in the future of K&F was Doc Kauffman. In early 1946, he traded his half of the company to Leo Fender for a punch press. Fender then formed the Fender Electric Instrument Company and introduced a new line of steels, including a doubleneck, and amps with natural or stained wood finishes—better looking and better made than the K&Fs. Fender continued to improve the electronics of his instruments. A trapezoid-shaped pickup with "strings-through" design (although the strings passed through magnets rather than the coil) that debuted in late 1948 would become one of Fender's most highly regarded lap steel pickups. In the summer of 1949, a budget-priced pearloid-covered model, the Champion, introduced an individual-pole piece pickup that would soon be found in the bridge position on Fender's classic Telecaster guitar.

Fender quickly became one of the more popular steel guitar brands, and the company continued to make steels and, later, pedal steels until 1980. Had Fender stayed exclusively with steels, however, the company might today be an obscure footnote to 1950s guitar history. Instead, Fender adapted the solidbody concept of the lap steel to the guitar and bass, and the guitar world would never be the same.

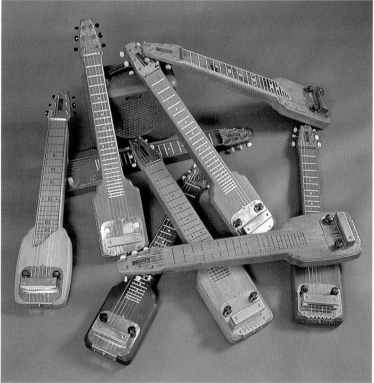

◀ K&F lap steels and amplifier, 1945. At a time when lap steel makers were trying to top each other with artistic body lines and color schemes, K&F took the low road with some of the plainest, cheapest-looking steels ever made. John Sprung/JS

▶ *Fender Dual 8 Professional, 1948. Fender's original singleneck models have six strings, but the first doubleneck has eight strings on each neck. In 1950 a Dual 6 Professional was added to the line. Gary Bohannon/WC*

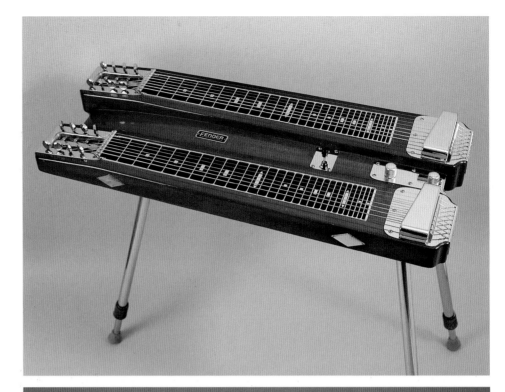

▶ *Fender Stringmaster, 1957. From 1950 to 1954 Fender brought forth three of the most important models in the history of the electric guitar: the Telecaster, Precision Bass, and Stratocaster. But even in this period of monumental achievement, Fender did not neglect its steel line. In 1953 the Stringmaster models debuted with a double-pickup system. The new pickup, in single or double configuration, would eventually be adopted on all steels and would also extend to some low-end guitar models. Gruhn Guitars/DL*

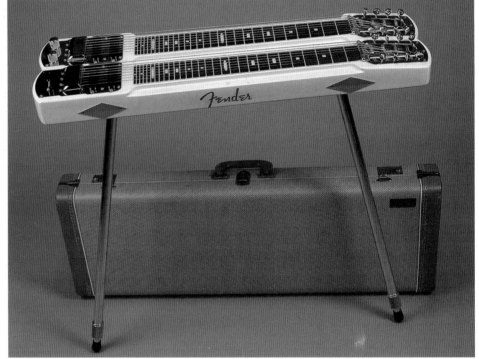

HAWAIIANS

▼   ▼   ▼

Other Makers

The lap steel guitar is one of the simplest and cheapest instruments to make. The only precision required involves positioning the nut and the saddle perpendicular to the strings. As long as the body is rigid, the sound quality depends almost entirely on the electronics. Consequently, lap steel designers have employed a great variety of materials, body shapes, and ornamentation styles.

Pitch-changing mechanisms had been in development since before the appearance of electric instruments, but until the 1950s players typically used pitch-changers only to retune. In 1954 Webb Pierce's recording of "Slowly" featured a pedal steel solo by Bud Isaacs, in which Isaacs changed pitch while the string was sounding. It was the death knell of the lap steel. The unique effect of changing one string while another one remained on the same pitch was possible only in very limited combinations on a lap steel, and musicians and makers alike turned their attention to pedal models.

The pedal steel market proved to be too small to compensate for the expense of designing and producing the instruments, and by the early 1970s almost all the major guitar makers were out of the steel guitar business, abandoning lap steels altogether and leaving pedal steels to smaller specialized companies. The market for lap steels in the 1980s was filled by dealers of vintage instruments, but demand had increased enough by the 1990s for the Matses company of West Boxford, Massachusetts, and the Morrell company of Bristol, Tennessee, to introduce new lap steel models.

▶ *Epiphone Varichord, circa 1940. Gibson's Electraharp, with six pedals, represented one way to change string pitch. In 1939, the same year the Electraharp appeared, Epiphone announced its own solution: pitch-changing levers built into the top. The Varichord's pitch-changers are incrementally calibrated, allowing a player to retune in a matter of seconds. Epiphone's catalog does not exaggerate much in claiming, "This instrument makes unheard of chordal possibilities possible. The only chord not obtainable is 'The Lost Chord.'" World War II halted production of this and almost all other Epi models, and, unlike Gibson, Epiphone did not emphasize steel guitars after the war. Walter Carter/WC*

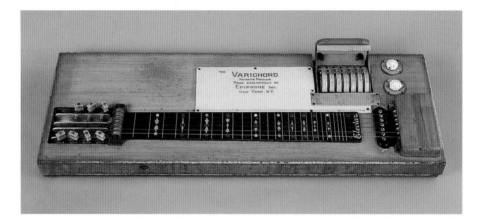

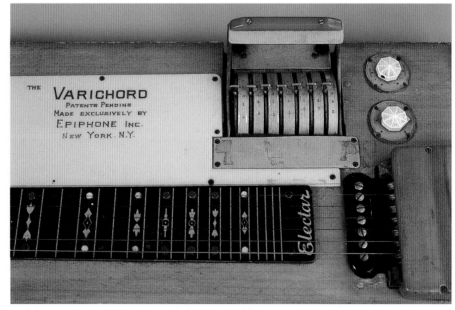

▼ Electrophone, late 1935. This is almost certainly the first electric model Epiphone brought to market in late 1935, and it appears the company was in a hurry. The neck, though square, looks like a neck blank for a standard guitar. Two body side pieces and three back pieces are glued on. The top is a piece of Bakelite, and the pickup is a close copy of Rickenbacker's. The colored dots on the fingerboard are typical of later Epi models. Mike Newton/MN

◀ Gretsch Electromatic, circa 1940. Like most companies, Gretsch led off its electric era with a lap steel. After World War II all Gretsch steels were made by Valco, but the maker of this prewar model is not clear. The tuner assembly (above) was made by the Harlin Brothers of Indianapolis, best known for the Multi-Kord pedal steel. Whoever it was, the manufacturer did not yet have a full complement of parts designed exclusively for an electric guitar. The mounting plate under the tone control (on the bass side) has settings that begin with 55, indicating that it was made for a radio tuner. Kyle Miller/WC

▲ Alkire E-Harp, made by Epiphone, early 1950s. Eddie Alkire of Easton, Pennsylvania, was one of the most famous steel guitarists of the prewar era. By 1941 he was playing a custom-made Rickenbacker 10-string Bakelite steel with a semichromatic tuning that made numerous harmonic combinations possible. In 1948 Alkire announced agreements with Epiphone, Gibson, and Rickenbacker to manufacture E-Harps, as he called them, and he also developed a mail-order business for E-Harp instructional books. Epiphone marketed this model by early 1952. Valco (National's parent company) was making an E-Harp covered in gray pearloid by 1954 and later made a console model finished in white. Gibson made a similar instrument, called the Century-10, but neither Gibson nor Rickenbacker ever made an Alkire E-Harp model. Gruhn Guitars/WC

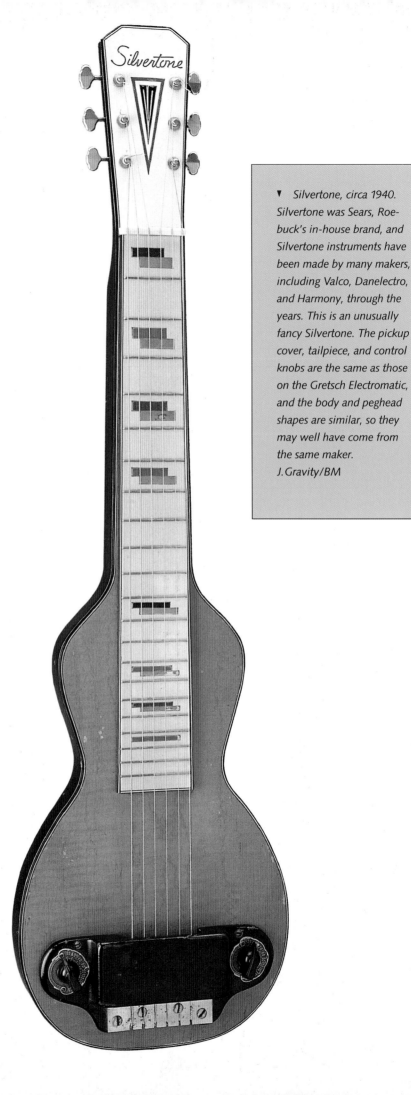

▼ Silvertone, circa 1940. Silvertone was Sears, Roebuck's in-house brand, and Silvertone instruments have been made by many makers, including Valco, Danelectro, and Harmony, through the years. This is an unusually fancy Silvertone. The pickup cover, tailpiece, and control knobs are the same as those on the Gretsch Electromatic, and the body and peghead shapes are similar, so they may well have come from the same maker. J. Gravity/BM

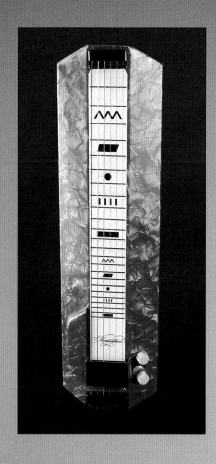

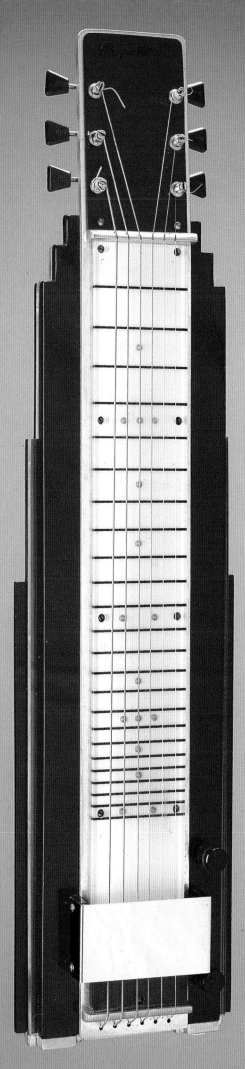

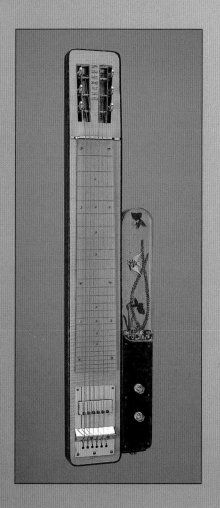

◄ *Magnatone, 1950s (above left). Magna Electronics of Inglewood, California, is probably best known for the Magnatone amp used by rock and roll legend Buddy Holly, but the company was also a strong competitor in the steel guitar market of the 1950s. The most common Magnatone lap steels are lightweight, pearloid-covered instruments with no visible pickup. In a foreshadowing of the Steinberger headless basses of the 1980s, this lap steel has tuners at the bridge and no peghead. Walter Carter/WC*

◄ *Premier "Aquarium," 1950s (below left). The Premier company of New York began making electric guitars and amps as early as 1939 and may be best remembered for scroll-body electric guitars of the 1960s. The aquarium scene on this lap steel has fish and plants embedded in clear plastic. Gordon Dow/BM*

▼ *Magnatone, 1950s. This large lap steel is made of alternating layers of clear and red plastic. Kyle Miller/BM*

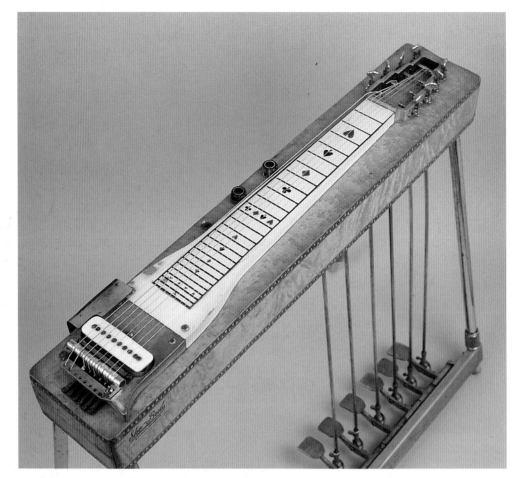

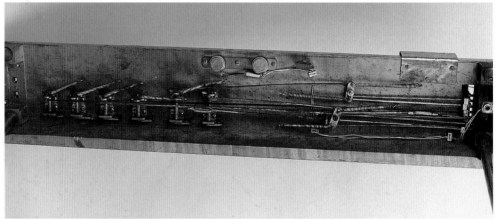

▲ *Melobar Powerslide 1-88, late 1980s. In 1970 Walter Smith of Weiser, Idaho, fixed all the "problems" of the standard lap steel. First, he attached a shoulder strap to allow a player to stand up and move around onstage. For an easier, more natural playing position he angled the plane of the neck away from the player. For accurate intonation he devised a notched guide (visible along the treble side of the fingerboard) to stop the steel at just the right spot. Eventually he attached plastic extension sleeves to the steel so that it could not be so easily dropped. In 1983 Smith offered soft body sides—foam covered with a variety of materials, including this fake cowhide. Smith died in 1990; his son Ted continues to make Melobars. This example has been refinished. Gruhn Guitars/WC*

◀ *Sho-Bud, circa 1959. Small companies specializing in pedal steels eventually took over the pedal steel market. One of the most successful was founded in Madison, Tennessee, in the late 1950s by musicians Shot Jackson and Buddy Emmons, who combined their first names into the company's name. The underside (below left) reveals the complicated system of rods and springs designed to "push" or "pull" (lower or raise pitch of) the strings. Joe Lacy/WC*

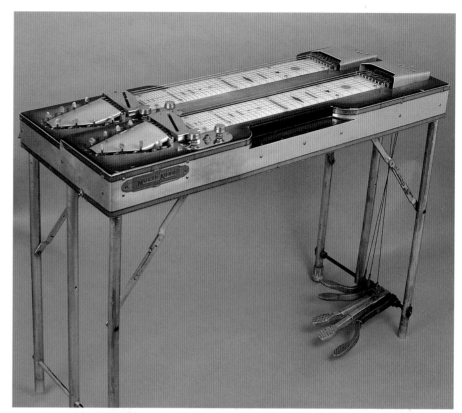

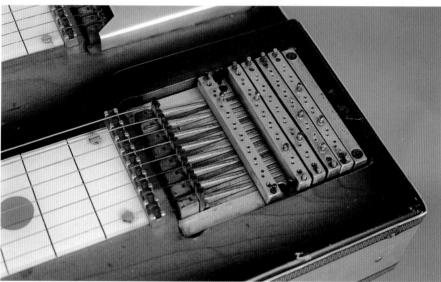

▲ *Harlin Brothers Multi-Kord, early 1950s. The Harlin Brothers of Indianapolis patented the double-finger, raise-and-lower pitch-changing mechanism (left) and prevented Gibson from using it. Despite the advanced design, most Multi-Kords were cheaply made and aimed at the student market. This sturdy model was designed for professional use. Gruhn Guitars/WC*

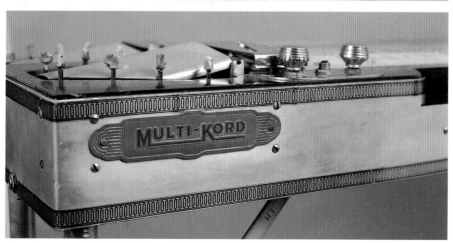

▶ *Vivi-Tone, 1933. Aside from the general body and neck lines and the sunburst finish, little about the Vivi-Tone electric Spanish guitar is conventional. The frets are much higher than standard, the soundhole has an odd shape, the bridge straddles the soundhole, the back is recessed and has f-holes. A pull-out drawer makes the electronics easily accessible. A pair of metal bridge posts rest on the metal strip that extends over the horseshoe magnet. When the strip is removed, the coil of wire surrounding one pole of the horseshoe is visible. John Sprung/JS*

SPANISH-NECKS
▼ ▼ ▼

Vivi-Tone

Vivi-Tone instruments are not nearly so famous or respected as the man who designed them, Lloyd Loar. A musician and acoustic engineer, Loar held the position of quality control supervisor at Gibson in the early 1920s. He helped design Gibson's Style 5 family of instruments, and F-5 mandolins bearing his signature of approval on the label are considered by players and collectors to be the finest instruments of their kind ever made.

By 1924 Loar had built an electric viola that he played in concert as well as a minimalist electric bass, but Gibson management was divided on the issue of electric instruments. The anti-electric faction won out, and by the end of 1924 not only Loar but Gibson general manager Lewis A. Williams and sales manager Clifford V. Buttleman had resigned.

To the conservative faction at Gibson, a company that in 1924 was playing catch-up in the tenor banjo market, Loar's vision may have seemed a mirage, but the electric instruments he saw on the horizon proved to be real— and not that far away. Within five years of Loar's departure, Stromberg-Voisinet and Vega introduced electrically amplified fretted instruments. Loar continued to work on new designs for electric and acoustic guitars along with various improvements for other instruments, including new bridges for pianos. By early 1933 his ideas were ready for market, and he formed the Vivi-Tone Company with his former Gibson associates.

Vivi-Tone launched the new guitars with a strong promotional campaign. In addition to advertisements, Lewis Williams placed a series of articles in *The Crescendo* magazine. Under the title "The Theory of Electrically Energized String Instruments" he detailed theories of acoustic and electric sound production. One article listed 16 reasons why a contact microphone was not suitable for an electric guitar—the first being that it would also pick up the player's sneezes, coughs, and private conversations—followed by 15 reasons why the "unit generator" (magnetic pickup) was better.

Advertisements claimed that Vivi-Tones were anywhere from 15 to 56 times louder than a conventional acoustic instrument. The company predicted doom for acoustic players with these futuristic headlines: "A larger crowd. A larger place. Harder to Cover. Poorer Acoustics. Fewer Players. Strings replaced by wind instruments. String Instrument Players were hanged on the hour. Efficient economy called for more power. Vivi-Tone asks, 'Why lose your job?'"

Another ad continued the pragmatic argument in catchy prose: "Is it a rational or irrational mind that argues for and protects weak, insipid efficiency; stands for auditorium half-coverage; and thus gives its player crutches instead of legs?... Managers are offering $5.00 more a night for Vivi-Tone. That's because they have found the stone-deaf enjoy the old type Gitar [*sic*] of the orchestra as well as you or I."

Unfortunately, Vivi-Tone guitars did not quite live up to advertising claims of power. Loar's pickup, developed back in his Gibson years, consisted essentially of multiple coils of wire wound around a magnet. When the instrument was played, the vibrations of the strings disturbed the magnetic field to produce an electric signal—the same basic principle used by Rickenbacker in 1932 and still the industry standard. But the implementation was significantly different—fatally so for Vivi-Tone. On a Vivi-Tone, the vibration of the strings was transferred through a wooden bridge to a metal bar that extended into the magnetic field. On a Rickenbacker the transfer went more directly from strings to magnetic field, with horseshoe-shaped magnets surrounding the strings plus individual pole pieces under the strings. Consequently, a Rickenbacker produced a much stronger signal than a Vivi-Tone.

Vivi-Tone did not fail simply because of a weak pickup, however. The company failed, in all probability, because *any* company that depended entirely on the sale of electric guitars in 1933 was bound to fail. Vivi-Tone's only real competitor, Ro-Pat-In, was an offshoot of Adolph Rickenbacker's successful tool and die business, a fortuitous situation since Ro-Pat-In sold only 95 guitar-amplifier sets in 1933. And most of these sales were Hawaiian guitars, which Vivi-Tone did not offer.

The overwhelming number of innovations that Vivi-Tone tried to implement all at once may have hastened its demise. Potential buyers may have been turned off by the sight of a bridge that seemed to be in the wrong place—straddling the soundhole. The acoustic model had a flat spruce back with *f*-holes, and the back was recessed into the body so that it could vibrate freely as a second sounding board. Frets were so high that the strings did not come into contact with the fingerboard. Some electric models had electronics mounted in a drawer that slid in and out of the side of the body. Patent drawings show a bridge system that could be adjusted to activate either the pickup for electric play or the back of the guitar for acoustic play. Other electrics did not have a back or sides; they were essentially the first solidbody electric guitars. To the playing public of 1933 the *idea* of electrification was hard enough to swallow; a guitar with a drawer full of electronics or no body at all was simply too much.

By the fall of 1933 Vivi-Tone was in financial trouble. On November 6, 1933, the company raised money by incorporating with $10,000 capital, but guitar production may have already been abandoned. The purpose of the new corporation, as announced in the December 1933 issue of *The Crescendo,* was to exploit Loar's invention of an electric keyboard instrument. The Vivi-Tone Clavier amplified the sound of metal tines that were struck by hammers—essentially the same system used in electric pianos made by Wurlitzer and Fender in the 1960s. The amplifier Vivi-Tone developed for the Clavier model was an electronic mammoth with 32 watts of power compared to the 3-watt output of the average amp of the day. But neither the Clavier nor the amp was successful.

Loar continued to believe in the potential of his guitar designs despite their commercial failure. He filed a patent application for the electric/acoustic guitar on January 27, 1934, and for the acoustic on May 14, 1934. Some Vivi-Tone ads referred to him as "Professor Loar," and he did, in fact, make his living from 1930 onward teaching at Northwestern University near Chicago. In 1943 he fell ill while performing on a YMCA-sponsored tour of France, and after returning to the United States he died on September 14, 1943.

▶ *Vivi-Tone electric mandolin, Acousti guitar, and electric mandocello, 1933. The mandolin (top) and mandocello (bottom) have an elongated body shape but appear to be standard f-hole models. The painted-on f-holes, however, suggest that something may be different, and the back view reveals that these instruments have no back or sides. They do have a pickup system—in a box rather than a drawer—that makes them the first electric solid-body fretted instruments. The guitar is Vivi-Tone's Acousti (acoustic) model. Roy Acuff Museum, Opryland USA/WC*

SPANISH-NECKS
▼ ▼ ▼

Solidbodies

The very first electric Hawaiian, Rickenbacker's Frying Pan, had a round neck and fret ridges, so the evolutionary step from the lap steel to the electric solidbody guitar seems like an easy, obvious one in hindsight. In reality, the step was huge. Whether it was due to lack of imagination among designers, lack of commitment from manufacturers, or—the most likely reason—the playing public's refusal to accept a radical new concept, the majority of solidbody guitars made before World War II looked more like variations on a Hawaiian theme than real Spanish-neck guitars. The solidbody electric would have to wait until the 1950s to secure its place in the guitar market.

▼ *Dobro All Electric, 1933.
This instrument looks very
much like a standard acoustic
Dobro (a hollowbody instrument), but it is more closely
related to a solidbody guitar
than to an amplified acoustic
instrument. Unlike Rickenbacker's electric Spanish
model of 1932, which is a
standard acoustic archtop
guitar with a pickup added,
this guitar has been gutted
of its acoustic capabilities.
Under the metal coverplate,
there is no sign of the resonator and "spider" bridge
that produce the acoustic
Dobro sound. Only the pickup appears, and it resembles
the one that would appear
on National-Dobro's metalbody lap steels in 1935. The
tuners have been reversed
for Hawaiian play, but with
a round neck and 14 frets
clear of the body, this guitar
was undoubtedly made for
standard playing. W. T.
Smith/WC*

▲ *Rickenbacker Electro
Spanish, circa 1936. Rickenbacker's Bakelite lap steel
(Model B) is one of the company's best-known models;
one of the more obscure is
this roundneck version of the
Bakelite model. The "Spanish" model was introduced at
about the same time as the
Hawaiian model, in mid-
1935, and both have hollow
areas under the metal plates
to reduce weight. The similarities extend to the 22 ¾-
inch scale length, which
makes this a "three-quarter"-
size guitar. Gruhn Guitars/BM*

◀ *Slingerland, circa 1939. The Slingerland company of Chicago, best known as a drum manufacturer, also made guitars and banjos. These apparent variations of the Songster Hawaiian model are actually two entirely different instruments. The slant of the bridge indicates that the guitar on the right is not a Hawaiian model at all but the Spanish-neck Songster referred to in the 1938 or 1939 catalog—the first production solidbody model from any maker prior to World War II that comes close to postwar solidbody design standards. The round-neck model has a longer scale (25 inches) and more frets clear of the body than the squareneck. The neck and center section of the body are a single piece of wood. The pickup includes individual string magnets as well as the large horseshoe, and the conflicting magnetic fields produce a signal with a slight tremolo effect. Gruhn Guitars/WC*

49

▼ *Rickenbacker Vibrola Spanish. Doc Kauffman, Leo Fender's early partner, invented a vibrola tailpiece that was fitted on the occasional 1930s Rickenbacker Electro Spanish (Bakelite model) and Gibson ES-150. In December 1937 Rickenbacker introduced this model with an internal electric motor (below right) that moves the tailpiece to change string pitch and create a vibrato effect. The device has one fundamental problem: If the motor is turned off at the low or high extreme of the vibrato, the guitar is then out of tune. A total of 90 Vibrola Spanish models were produced. Gruhn Guitars/WC*

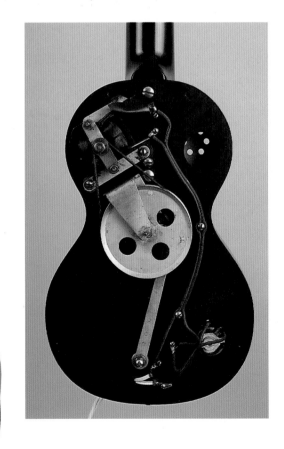

◄ *Les Paul "Log," circa 1940 (opposite page top). By the late 1930s the greater sustaining power of a solidbody guitar over a guitar with a vibrating top had become common knowledge among guitarists, thanks to the popularity of electric Hawaiian models. To maximize sustain, entertainer Les Paul anchored the vital parts of an electric guitar on a 4" x 4" piece of pine. The body "wings" are from an Epiphone archtop and are strictly cosmetic. The peghead and neck are Gibson-made, although the tuners are from an Epiphone and the inlay pattern on the fingerboard indicates that it was made by the Larson brothers of Chicago. Paul made the pickups, bridge, and vibrato unit (left) himself. The hole in the top near the control knobs is a mystery; even Paul cannot remember what went there. He played "The Log," as it was nicknamed, in public in the 1940s, but no manufacturers showed interest in it. Country Music Hall of Fame Collection/WC*

▲ *Bigsby, circa 1947. Country music star Merle Travis commissioned this guitar from Paul Bigsby, the man whose name is found on tailpiece vibrato units from the 1950s on. Had Bigsby of Downey, California, gone into production with his guitars, he would probably be known today as the father of the electric solidbody (he is known as the father of the modern pedal steel), but he made only a handful. After 1950 he referred customers for solidbody guitars to Leo Fender. Country Music Hall of Fame Collection/WC*

◀ *App, 1942. In the winter of 1941–42 O. W. Appleton of Burlington, Iowa, made what is undoubtedly the first solidbody guitar with a carved top. "App" put a Gibson neck on this guitar and tried to interest Gibson in it. Gibson passed, but when the first Gibson solidbody was introduced in 1952 it was remarkably similar. The App was somewhat thicker than the new Gibson—three inches at the sides (three-and-a-half inches in the middle of the body) compared with two inches for the Gibson—and a half-inch wider across the lower bout (13½ inches compared to 13 inches). The most significant difference, so far as Appleton was concerned, was on the peghead, where instead of "App," the Gibson said "Les Paul Model." Appleton did not make many instruments, and he eventually retired to Nogales, Arizona. Country Music Hall of Fame Collection/WC*

SPANISH-NECKS

▼ ▼ ▼

Hollowbodies

To the playing public of the 1930s an electric guitar had to look like a guitar and not just a plank of wood with electronics and a guitar neck attached. All commercially successful electric models prior to World War II were essentially standard acoustic guitars—the great majority of them archtops—with a pickup mounted into the top.

▼ *National Style O, 1938, with Silvo electronics. National offered the electronics assembly of the Silvo Hawaiian model as a conversion kit for the Style O or any other model with a single-cone resonator. The black disc fits neatly into the hole that held the coverplate and resonator; a jack mounted into the side of the instrument completes the electric conversion. Gruhn Guitars/WC*

◀ *National Electric Spanish, circa 1938. The earliest version of the Electric Spanish, introduced in 1935, has standard f-holes. National, a company with a reputation for innovation, found a way to modernize this model while still maintaining a conventional archtop look. In 1936 the soundholes in the top were eliminated. The two-piece blade pickup (above) is similar to that of National's first lap steels. Cohn Rude/BM*

▲ *Gibson ES-150, 1938. Unlike National, which entered the electric market with a classy-looking model, Gibson debuted in 1936 with a rather plain guitar. The body is 16¼ inches wide with a flat back—hardly in the same league with Gibson's 17- and 18-inch acoustic archtops. The pickup is so heavy that many examples have two posts inside to support the top. The guitar was marketed with an amplifier for $150, hence the model name ES-150 (ES for Electric Spanish). Pioneer electric guitarist Charlie Christian played an ES-150 and Gibson's more expensive ES-250. Many players still consider the "Christian" bar pickup to be the quintessential jazz pickup and the ES-150 and ES-250 the best prewar electrics from any maker. Gibson kept the pickup as an option in the 1950s and made it standard on a special model, the ES-175CC (CC for Charlie Christian), in 1978 and 1979. The vibrato was designed by Doc Kauffman. Gruhn Guitars/WC*

▲ Gibson ES-150, circa 1941. The ES-150 was upgraded with an arched back and a new pickup in 1940. The postwar ES-150 sported a wider 17-inch body, but newer styles with cutaway body shapes and multiple pickups quickly overtook the ES-150, and it was discontinued in 1956. Gruhn Guitars/WC

▲ Gibson ES-100, 1938. By 1938 the ES-150 was selling well enough for Gibson to add a lower model and a higher model to the line. The ES-100 is 14 ¼ inches wide and has a plainer pickup. With its companion amplifier, it sold for $100. It was given a new pickup and renamed ES-125 in 1941, revamped again after World War II, and last made in 1969. Gruhn Guitars/WC

◀ Gibson ES-250, 1939. The ES-250, made only from 1938 to 1940, was the company's first high-end electric guitar. Its 17-inch body width, fancy inlay, and stairstep peghead shape put it in a class with Gibson's better acoustic archtop models. Charlie Christian is pictured with this model in a Gibson catalog photo. Gruhn Guitars/DD

▼ Gibson ES-300, 1940. With the introduction of the ES-300 in 1940, Gibson debuted yet another pickup and a new peghead ornament. This huge, 6¾-inch unit lasted only a few months before it was replaced with a smaller but similar unit. The "crown" on the peghead did last and is found today on many of Gibson's higher models. Like the high-end acoustic archtops, the ES-300 was available with natural finish. As befits an expensive guitar, the maple back has a highly figured "tiger-stripe" grain. Crawford White/WC

▶ *Gibson ETB, 1939 (far right). By the late 1930s Gibson offered an electric tenor banjo, plectrum banjo, five-string banjo, and mandolin. Whereas the electric guitars and mandolin are essentially acoustic models with electronics added, the ETB, EPB, and ERB (for Electric Tenor, Plectrum, and Regular Banjo, respectively) have only the neck of a standard banjo. There is no banjo-style head (a skin head would not carry the weight of a pickup), rim, or resonator. Instead, the body is built like a Gibson lap steel with a thick wood top and a screwed-on back (near right). The tailpiece includes a palm-pressure vibrato. The banjo was past its heyday by 1939, and electric banjos fared even worse than acoustics. They were not revived in the Gibson line after World War II. Gruhn Guitars/WC*

▶ *Gibson ES-300, 1940. Within a few months of the ES-300's debut this smaller oblong pickup appeared. Although this guitar has a later serial number than the example shown with the larger pickup, this body has an earlier factory work-order number. All Gibson electric production was stopped in mid-1942 for World War II, and none of the prewar pickup styles except for the Charlie Christian appeared on postwar guitars. Gruhn Guitars/WC*

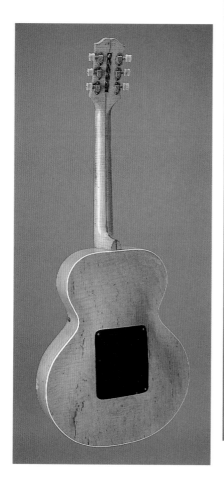

◄ Epiphone Zephyr, circa 1941. Epiphone introduced the Zephyr as its fanciest electric in 1939. Epiphone employee Herb Sunshine designed the electric guitar line, including the adjustable-pole pickup. Easy access to electronics is not a problem on a prewar Epiphone, thanks to a large hole in the back. Miessner Inventions, Inc., of Milburn, New Jersey, held patents on electronic keyboard instruments and claimed that the same patents covered electric guitars. Epiphone paid a licensing fee and put patent notices on instruments, but other companies stood up to Miessner's legal threats, and the claims were eventually dropped or settled. Lloyd Chiate/BM

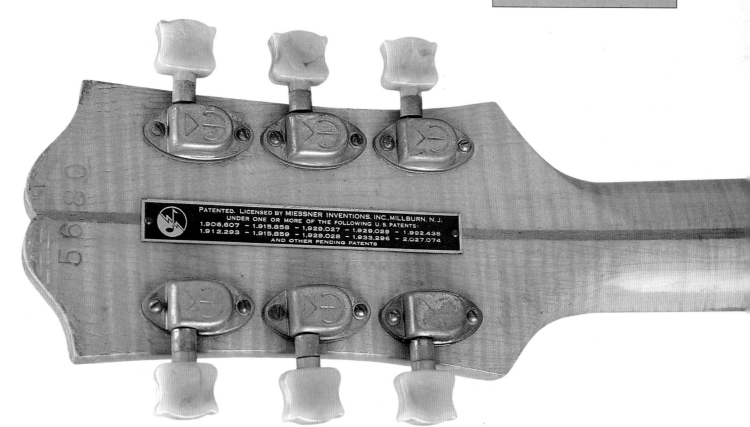

PATENTED. LICENSED BY MIESSNER INVENTIONS, INC., MILLBURN. N.J.
UNDER ONE OR MORE OF THE FOLLOWING U.S. PATENTS:
1,906,607 – 1,915,858 – 1,929,027 – 1,929,029 – 1,992,438
1,912,293 – 1,915,859 – 1,929,028 – 1,933,296 – 2,027,074
AND OTHER PENDING PATENTS

▶ *Rickenbacker Electro Mandolin, Electro Tenor Guitar, and amplifier, mid 1930s. Acoustic tenor guitars were popular in the early 1930s, but electric tenors never caught on. This early version of Rickenbacker's electric mandolin has the company's horseshoe pickup mounted on a rough approximation of a standard mandolin body. But any resemblance to a standard mandolin is for cosmetic purposes only; with a flat top, no soundholes, and an all-mahogany body, this instrument was never intended to have any significant acoustic properties. In the late 1930s Rickenbacker redesigned the model with a more conventional carved spruce top and maple back and sides, but it still did not last through World War II. John Sprung/JS*

▲ *Vega tenor, circa 1939. The pickup on this electric tenor guitar appears to be a copy of Rickenbacker's horseshoe type, but the "horseshoe" magnets are only half-horseshoes. When removed, they reveal a double-coil pickup. The coils are wound in reverse so as to be hum-canceling. Gibson "introduced" the same feature with its humbucking pickups of 1957. Mike Larko/WC*

PART TWO
▼ ▼ ▼

Branches of the Electric Family:
1947 to the 1990s

World War II caused more than just an interruption of production in the guitar industry. When the war ended most companies could not simply pick up where they had left off, for the market they faced had changed. Electric guitars, which had been barely out of the experimental stage prior to the war, quickly became dominant. National/Valco, the company that had invented acoustic resonator guitars in the late 1920s, shifted its focus to electrics after the war and never again produced any quality resonator instruments. Gibson, which had established and reigned over the market for acoustic archtop guitars before the war, concentrated on electrics in the late 1940s, refining pickup designs and expanding the electric line. Gretsch and Epiphone saw electrics as the future and shifted emphasis accordingly. Fender, the most innovative company of the late 1940s and early 1950s, had not even existed before the war. Of the major manufacturers, only the tradition-minded Martin company stayed its course, continuing through the 1950s to concentrate on the style of guitar that had been the company's calling card since its founding in 1833—acoustic flat tops.

The increasing demand for electric guitars made competition among makers fierce, which in turn led to a deluge of innovations from the late 1940s to the late 1950s. By the dawn of the 1960s the electric guitar could claim a limb, with three distinct branches, on the tree of fretted instrument evolution. The same three basic styles of electric guitar endure today: the archtop hollowbody, the solidbody, and the hybrid semi-hollowbody style combining elements from archtop and solidbody designs.

FULL-DEPTH HOLLOWBODIES
▼ ▼ ▼

Gibson

After World War II Gibson resumed production determined to dominate the electric guitar market. The three models from 1942—ES-125, ES-150, and ES-300—were revived with upgrades, including larger bodies for the ES-125 and ES-150 and new pickups on all three. By 1951 the electric line had grown to 10 models, some of them sporting multiple-pickup systems and cutaway body styles. Gibson seemed to be at the forefront of electric guitar design, but concep-

▲ *Gibson ES-150, 1950. After World War II Gibson updated its original electric Spanish-neck model, the ES-150, with a wider, 17-inch body and a new pickup, the P-90. The single-coil unit with adjustable pole pieces became one of the most respected pickups in the guitar industry and appeared for more than 40 years on various Gibson models. Curiously, the ES-150 of the late 1940s has an unbound fingerboard with dot inlay, while the lower-grade ES-125 of the same period has trapezoidal inlay. In 1949 the inlay patterns on the two models were swapped. Gruhn Guitars/DL*

tually the company was stuck in the prewar period, when manufacturers believed that the public would only buy electric guitars that looked like acoustic guitars. Some of Gibson's electrics were made of laminated rather than solid pieces of wood, but all of Gibson's 1951 electrics—nine *f*-hole archtops and one flat top—were conventional acoustic guitars with electronics added.

Gibson's concept of a commercial electric guitar changed quickly when Fender's solidbody electrics, introduced in mid 1950, immediately gained a share of the market. In 1952 Gibson turned its attention away from full-depth hollowbodies and challenged Fender with the first of an entire line of solidbody models endorsed by recording star Les Paul. In 1958 Gibson combined elements of hollow- and solidbody design into a successful new style, the thinbody semi-hollow electric guitar. By the end of the decade solidbody and semi-hollow guitars had surpassed full-depth archtops in popularity.

The decline of the full-depth archtop was not absolute. As public tastes shifted to other styles, the low-end full-depth archtop did indeed pass into history, and the market share held by the surviving models shrank considerably. However, in numbers of instruments, high-quality electric archtops maintained fairly steady sales, and the full-depth archtop continues to be the guitar of choice for many jazz players today.

◀ *Gibson ES-350/ES-5 prototype, 1949. This guitar is labeled "ES-350," but the ES-350 started out in 1947 with a single pickup and gained only one additional pickup in 1948. A three-pickup archtop—the only one ever offered under the Gibson brand—would be introduced later in 1949 as the ES-5. Although the pickups are standard P-90s, the covers appear to have been handcut and bent rather than molded (left). The tailpiece, the A-string tuner button, several fingerboard dots, and the metal button in the pickguard are not original. James Harman/WC*

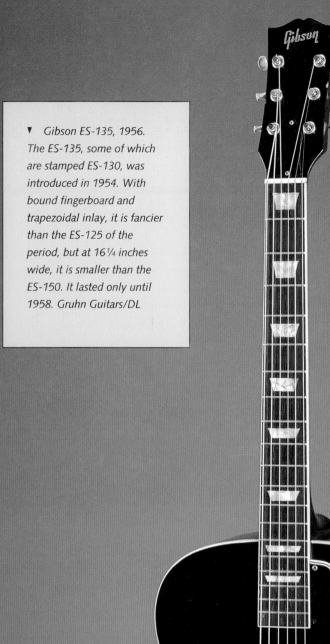

▼ *Gibson ES-135, 1956. The ES-135, some of which are stamped ES-130, was introduced in 1954. With bound fingerboard and trapezoidal inlay, it is fancier than the ES-125 of the period, but at 16¼ inches wide, it is smaller than the ES-150. It lasted only until 1958. Gruhn Guitars/DL*

▲ *Gibson ES-300, circa 1947. The most expensive prewar electric is still appealing in its postwar form—particularly with a new f-hole tailpiece—but its reign at the top of the line was short-lived. A cutaway version, the ES-350, provided competition, and both models were soon overshadowed by electric versions of the high-end acoustic archtops. The ES-300 was discontinued in 1952. Megatar/BM*

▲ Gibson L-7ED, 1949. Because of the laminated construction of Gibson electrics, they were considered inferior to the company's acoustic models by some players. In 1948 Gibson came up with a way for players to electrify an acoustic archtop and still maintain its acoustic qualities. The "fingerrest" pickup, more commonly known by the name of its designer, Gibson president Ted McCarty, contained all the electronics in the pickguard. The unit was offered as an accessory for any archtop model, but the L-7 (Gibson's cheapest 17-inch model) with McCarty pickup was cataloged as a separate model: the L-7E with one pickup or the L-7ED with two pickups. A true electric L-7 was never offered. Gruhn Guitars/WC

▼ Gibson ES-5, 1950. The ES-5, introduced in 1949, was the first Gibson electric to break the price-based system of model names. The 5 in the model name refers to Gibson's highly regarded L-5 acoustic archtop. At a time when few electric models had even two pickups, this ES-5 sports three. The control system is unusual by modern standards but consistent with Gibson's two-pickup models: a volume control for each pickup, no pickup selector switch, and a master tone control (on the cutaway bout of this model). Gary Dick/BM

▼ Gibson ES-5 Switchmaster, 1956. The ES-5's limited tone/volume control system was revamped in late 1955 with the addition of individual pickup tone controls and a four-position pickup selector switch that inspired the addition of "Switchmaster" to the model name. The tune-o-matic bridge with individually adjustable saddles had been introduced by Gibson in 1954, and it became standard on the ES-5 in 1955. A fancier tailpiece appeared in 1956. Although this guitar has the prestigious Style 5 designation, the wood grain of the back is rather plain compared with that of a classic L-5 acoustic or even some other ES-5 examples. The ES-5 was discontinued in 1962. Gruhn Guitars/WC

▼ *Gibson ES-175, 1952. A pointed cutaway shape distinguishes Gibson's first small-bodied (16¼-inch) cutaway electric from the larger models. The ES-175 debuted in 1949 with a single pickup. A double-pickup version appeared in 1953 and became one of Gibson's most successful models. The single-pickup ES-175 was discontinued in 1971 but the ES-175D is still in production. Clifford Antone/BM*

▲ *Gibson ES-175D custom plectrum, 1955. Gibson did not catalog any plectrum guitars after World War II, but virtually anything was available by custom order. The "bow-tie" inlay is a standard banjo inlay of the period. The P-90 pickups have full-size (six-string) covers but only four poles. Otherwise, this is a standard ES-175. Strings West Tulsa/BM*

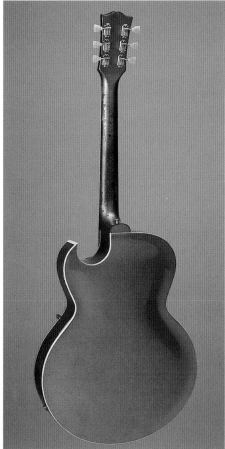

◀ Gibson ES-175DN, 1957 (far left). Though priced in the middle range, the ES-175 received high-end treatment in 1957 when it was fitted with Gibson's new double-coil humbucking pickups. Joe Lacy/DL

◀ Gibson ES-140, 1952 (near left). Gibson introduced a three-quarter-size acoustic flat top guitar in 1949 and followed it with this three-quarter-size version of the ES-175 a year later. The ES-140 has a 22¾-inch scale and a 12¾-inch body width. Annual sales averaged 300 instruments until 1957, when it was replaced by a thinbody version. The ES-140T was equally successful but discontinued in 1960. Gruhn Guitars/WC

◀ Gibson ES-295, 1956. In 1952 Gibson introduced two models with gold finish. The hollowbody is essentially a fancy ES-175 with white pickup covers, a floral-painted pickguard, and gold-plated hardware. The trapeze-style combination bridge-tailpiece is the same as that of the gold-finish solidbody, the Les Paul Model, except that the strings wrap under the tailpiece on the Les Paul. The gold finish extends to the back, sides, and neck of the ES-295 (far left); the great majority of gold Les Pauls have gold finish on the top only. The ES-295 was discontinued in 1959. Jim Colclasure/BM

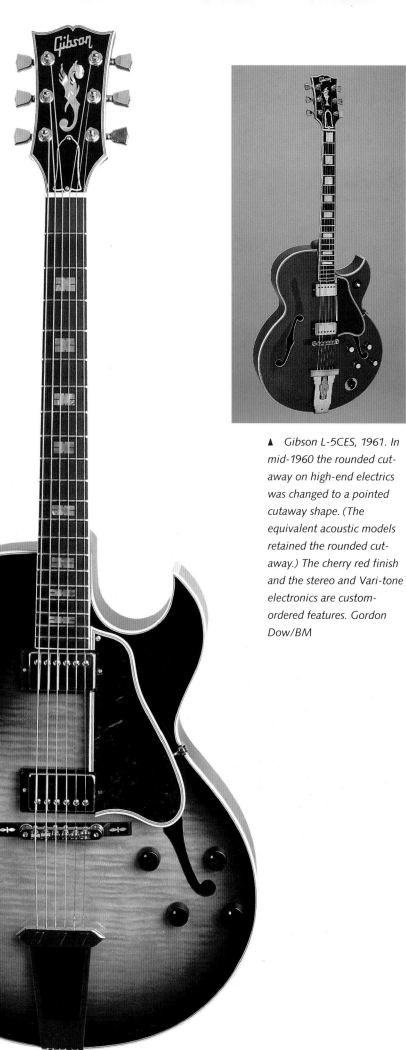

▼ Gibson ES-775, 1991. This fancy version of the ES-175 sports gold-plated hardware, a bound tortoise-grain pickguard, and wood knobs. The slotted-block fingerboard inlays, not found on any other Gibson model, appear on several Epiphone models from 1937 through the 1960s. Gruhn Guitars/WC

▲ Gibson L-5CES, 1961. In mid-1960 the rounded cut-away on high-end electrics was changed to a pointed cutaway shape. (The equivalent acoustic models retained the rounded cut-away.) The cherry red finish and the stereo and Vari-tone electronics are custom-ordered features. Gordon Dow/BM

◀ *Gibson L-5CES left-handed, 1952. Gibson introduced a true electric version of the L-5C (cutaway) with solid carved top and solid back and sides in 1951. Unlike the ES-5, which was inspired by the L-5 but has a body of laminated wood, this model is an L-5 that has been fitted with pickups. It should properly be called the ES-5 or ES-5C, but since that name was already taken, Gibson put the ES after the model name: L-5CES. The wood grain of the back (far left) is worthy of the Style 5 name. Gruhn Guitars/WC*

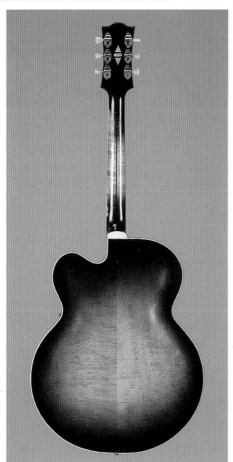

◀ *Gibson Super 400CES, 1951. Gibson's top-of-the-line acoustic archtop, the 18-inch-wide Super 400C (cutaway) appeared in an electric version introduced along with the L-5CES in 1951. Joseph Nuyens/DL*

▶ Gibson Super 400CES custom seven-string, 1953, with EA-400 amplifier, 1959. This guitar was custom ordered with three pickups but no controls on the guitar. The output jack, a "cannon" microphone type, keeps each pickup on a separate channel. Tone and volume controls are housed in a box with three standard outputs. The original owner played through three amplifiers. (At one point, he added a fourth pickup and played through four amps.) In 1957 Gibson introduced the EA-400, a three-channel amp that seems to have been designed just for this guitar. Bill Banks/WC

▶ Gibson Super 400CESN, 1956. This instrument was owned by Scotty Moore, who played it on numerous Elvis Presley records. It sports Gibson's high-end pickup of the mid-1950s, known by the trade name for the magnets, Alnico V. These pickups are distinguishable from the P-90s by their rectangular, non-adjustable pole pieces (center). The back (far right) shows an unusual "blistered" wood grain. Chips Moman/WC

▼ *Gibson Super 400CES custom, 1960. This guitar was modeled after a Super 400 custom made for entertainer Merle Travis. The Bigsby vibrato was a standard Gibson option at the time, and the banjo-style armrest is a feature of many of Travis's guitars. The pointed cutaway shape had just been implemented on Gibson's high-end electric archtops. Among the unique features of the peghead ornamentation is a non-standard The Gibson logo. The back and neck are of nicely figured maple. Johnny R. Chamelin/DL*

▲ Gibson Super 400CES, 1960. Black was never an official custom color for any Gibson full-depth electric archtop. In various periods throughout the company's history, however, black was used to cover cosmetic imperfections in wood. Here it sets off the gold-plated metal parts of this guitar. Clifford Antone/BM

▲ Gibson Super 400CES, 1963. In the 1960s a natural-finish Super 400CES listed for only $25 more than a sunburst, but the natural finish is much rarer—141 shipped from 1961 through 1969 compared with 368 sunbursts. Lloyd Chiate/BM

◀ Gibson Super 300CES, 1961. In the acoustic line the Super 300 is a plain version of the 18-inch Super 400. No electric counterpart was ever cataloged or noted on shipping records, but this one was built—and labeled "Super 300CES"—never-theless. The vibrato is not original. John Brinkman/WC

Gibson Johnny Smith
Double, 1965. Jazz guitarist
Johnny Smith endorsed a
Guild in the 1950s, then
moved to Gibson in 1961.
His namesake model in the
Gibson line is a fully
acoustic guitar with a solid
carved top and "floating"
pickups. It has the body size,
X-pattern top bracing, and
25-inch scale (none standard
Gibson specifications) of
Smith's personal D'Angelico
guitar. Gibson introduced a
single-pickup Johnny Smith
in 1961, followed by the
double-pickup model in
1963. It remained Gibson's
top "artist" model until
Smith's endorsement agreement ended in 1989.
Gordon Dow/BM

Gibson Barney Kessel
Regular, 1967. Jazz musician
Barney Kessel signed on with
Gibson in 1961 after an
association with Kay. The
double pointed cutaways of
the Gibson Kessels are
unusual on a full-depth
guitar. Otherwise, the electronics and ornamentation
are standard Gibson. A total
of 1,069 Barney Kessel Reg-
ulars were shipped through
1970. Gruhn Guitars/DL

◀ Gibson Barney Kessel
Custom, 1964. The fancier
Kessel model is the only
Gibson catalog model ever
to have a musical note as a
peghead ornament. The
bow-tie fingerboard pattern,
unique among Gibson guitar
models, is a standard banjo
pattern. The Kessel Custom
was not so successful as
the Regular, with shipments
of 722 guitars from 1961
through 1970. Fret Ware/BM

▼ *Gibson Tal Farlow, 1964.
The third jazz artist to sign
with Gibson in the early
1960s, Tal Farlow, endorsed
one of the more unusually
ornamented Gibson electric
archtops. It is also one of the
rarest, with a total of 215
made between 1962 and
1967. The fingerboard inlays
are an upside-down version
of the "crest" pattern of
Gibson's J-200 flat top.
On the peghead, a second
"crown" is inlaid in an
upside-down position.
Unlike the body scroll of
Gibson's F-style mandolins,
the Tal Farlow's scroll is
merely suggested by inlaid
binding material rather than
cut into the body. Gibson
debuted a new shade of
sunburst finish on this model
and called it "viceroy
brown." The light brown
shading enhances the wood
grain of the maple neck.
Gold Dust/BM*

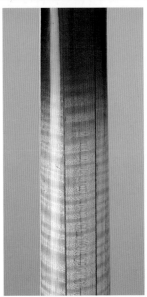

◄ *Gibson Trini Lopez Deluxe, 1964 (far left). Nightclub singer Trini Lopez was not noted for his guitar work, but in 1964 he was about the only artist of the folk music boom who played an electric. His two Gibson endorsement models are quite different. The Lopez Deluxe has the same body style as a Barney Kessel but with a standby switch (standard on Gretsch models of the period but unheard-of on a Gibson) on the upper bass bout. The less expensive Trini Lopez Standard is a thinline model based on the ES-335. Both Lopez models are distinguished by diamond-shaped soundholes and a peghead with six-on-a-side tuners. The peghead on this example is very unusual, with banjo-type tuners and "reverse" shape (tuners on the bass side)— features found only on Gibson's Firebird solidbody models of the same year. Sales of Lopez Deluxes through 1970 totaled 303. Shane's/BM*

▼ *Gibson Tal Farlow, 1964. Cherry sunburst is common on Gibsons of the 1960s but quite unusual on a Tal Farlow. Clifford Antone/BM*

▶ Gibson ES-335TD custom, circa 1969. The three-inch body depth of this guitar belies the T (for Thinbody) in the model name. The double-rounded cutaway body shape and the electronics are those of the thin-line ES-335, but this instrument is more likely an early version of the ES-150DC. Eldon Proffitt/WC

▼ Gibson ES-150DCN, 1969. This new model of 1969 bears little resemblance to the ES-150s made from 1936 to 1956. Its name came, no doubt, from its list price, which fell between those of the ES-175D and the ES-125. The standard ES-150DC (DC for Double Cutaway) has Gibson's usual four knobs and pickup selector switch, but it also has a master tone control on the upper treble bout—the only double-pickup Gibson model with this feature. Clifford Antone/BM

◄ Gibson CF-100E, 1954 (far left). Gibson introduced its first cutaway flat top, the CF-100, in an electric as well as an acoustic version in 1950. The pickup on the CF-100E is small and mounted unobtrusively at the end of the fingerboard. Like the acoustic version, the electric has an X-braced top so that much of the acoustic sound is retained. The model only lasted until 1959. Gruhn Guitars/WC

◄ Gibson J-160E, 1955. This jumbo-body electric flat top debuted in 1954 with the added attraction of an adjustable-height bridge. The larger, non-cutaway body should have given it a bigger sound than the smaller CF-100E, but the top is laminated and the bracing is lateral or "ladder" style rather than X-pattern, resulting in an inferior acoustic sound. Its association with John Lennon of the Beatles helped keep it in the line until 1979. It was reissued in 1991 with a solid, X-braced top. Gruhn Guitars/WC

FULL-DEPTH HOLLOWBODIES
▼ ▼ ▼

Epiphone

In the years immediately following World War II Epiphone provided Gibson with the same formidable competition that it had before the war. Like Gibson, Epiphone introduced improved electronics and attractive new electric models—full-depth archtops. Unlike Gibson, however, Epiphone was in financial trouble by the early 1950s. In 1953 the Stathopoulo family, who had owned the company from its founding in 1873, sold to C. G. Conn, the prominent band instrument manufacturer and Epi's distributor since 1935. Probably to avoid unionization of the Epi factory in New York, Conn began moving production to Philadelphia. Stathopoulo family members regained control in 1955 but were unable to resume full-scale production.

Epiphone made one line of highly respected instruments with no post-war competition from Gibson—acoustic basses. Epi's impending demise in the mid 1950s prompted Gibson president Ted McCarty to go after Epi's bass manufacturing equipment. (Gibson had made basses, as well as violas, violins, and cellos, from 1940 to 1942, but apparently the company no longer had the tooling.) In 1957 Gibson's parent corporation, the Chicago Musical Instrument Co., bought not only Epi's bass production equipment but the entire Epiphone inventory of guitars, parts, and equipment, along with the Epiphone name, for $20,000. Epiphone was reincorporated and operated essentially as a branch of Gibson.

Gibson introduced a full line of acoustic and electric Epiphone guitars and upright basses in 1958. They sported pickups, necks, and other parts from the Epi factory inventory as well as model names of older Epis, but the electric line did *not* represent a continuation of the Epiphone tradition. Of the five electric archtops, only the Broadway had a full-depth body; the other four were thinlines. Only one other full-depth Epi electric hollowbody emerged during the period when Gibson made Epis in America: the Howard Roberts, which was introduced in 1964, discontinued along with the Broadway when production was moved to Japan in 1970, and eventually revived under the Gibson brand.

▸ *Epiphone Zephyr De Luxe Regent, 1951. These smaller pickups are standard on most Epis from 1951 to 1961. Although the guitars themselves may have been made in Philadelphia, Kalamazoo, or New York, collectors call these "New York" pickups. Gruhn Guitars/WC*

▲ Epiphone Zephyr De Luxe Regent, circa 1950. "Regent" in an Epi model name denotes a cutaway body. The Zephyr De Luxe Regent debuted by 1949 an electric cutaway version of the De Luxe. The top is laminated spruce; the back and sides are laminated maple. These large pickups appear on this model only around 1949 and 1950. Gruhn Guitars/DL

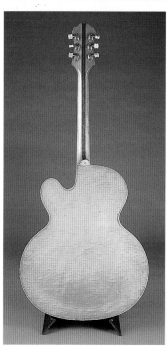

◀ Epiphone Zephyr Emperor Regent, circa 1954 (far left). The electric cutaway version of Epiphone's 18 1/2-inch Emperor model debuted by 1952. To elevate it a step above the De Luxe, Epi put three pickups and a push-button selector system on the Emperor. By the time this guitar was made, a laminated maple top had replaced the spruce top of earlier models. Also, the truss rod adjustment was moved from the body end of the neck to the peghead in 1952. As befits a top-of-the-line model, the back shows a nice curly maple grain. Danny Henderson/DL

◀ Epiphone Emperor, 1961 (near left). The standard Gibson-made Emperor electric is a thinbody guitar. This full-depth Emperor was custom made from what appears to be the body of an acoustic Emperor (the top is spruce rather than maple) and a leftover Epiphone-made neck from 1957 or earlier. All standard Emperors—whether Epi-made or Gibson-made—have three pickups. This oddity has just two pickups and a master volume control, another nonstandard feature. Gruhn Guitars/WC

▲ Epiphone Zephyr Cutaway, mid 1950s. The Zephyr model was the top of the line when it was introduced in 1939 but had become a midline model by the time this guitar was made. Although the cutaway version is listed in catalogs as Zephyr Regent, this guitar is labeled more directly: Zephyr Cutaway. This type of DeArmond pickup, usually associated with Gretsch models of the period, is original equipment on some Epiphones. Gruhn Guitars/BM

▶ Epiphone Harry Volpe models, 1956. Although the De Luxe and Emperor brought Epiphone a high degree of respect, the company needed a low-end model in the mid 1950s to increase sales. Despite the endorsement by well-known jazz player Harry Volpe, who had often been pictured in the late 1930s and early 1940s with a fancy Gretsch archtop, this model was designed for the student market, featuring extra-wide string spacing for easier play. The pickups are the type found on Epi's larger (16 3/8 inches wide) Century model. The knobs on the sunburst example are not original. Gruhn Guitars/WC

▼ *Epiphone Broadway, 1960. When Gibson unveiled its Epiphone line in 1958, four of the five electric arch-top models—Emperor, Broadway, Century, and Zephyr—were named after previous Epi models (Shera-ton was the new name), but the guitars themselves were quite different from the pre-Gibson models. All except the Broadway became thin-bodies in the Gibson line. The Broadway, although it had been a highly respected acoustic model, had never before been available in an electric version. Lloyd Chiate/BM*

▲ *Epiphone Broadway custom, 1968. This guitar is labeled with a Broadway model number, E-252, but it is hardly a 17 3/8-inch guitar with a rounded cutaway. The body is that of Gibson's 16 1/4-inch model, the ES-175. Perhaps the customer pre-ferred the Epiphone appointments or the mini-humbucking pickups to those of the standard ES-175. Gruhn Guitars/WC*

◄ Epiphone Howard Roberts Custom, circa 1965. This fancier version of the Howard Roberts, with a more ornate peghead and a tune-o-matic bridge, joined the line in 1965. Both models were discontinued when Gibson moved Epi production to Japan in 1970. The Custom was revived with a laminated maple top, among other changes, under the Gibson brand from 1974 through 1980. Tommy Goldsmith/DL

▼ Epiphone Howard Roberts, 1965. Jazz player Howard Roberts designed this model after observing that on a standard f-hole archtop, the pickguard covers most of the treble-side hole and the player's arm covers the bass-side hole. To maximize acoustic qualities, he specified an oval hole and a floating pickup (like that used on Gibson's Johnny Smith model). Curiously, despite Roberts's concern for acoustics, the tone and volume controls are mounted into the top rather than on the pickguard. The model debuted with a cherry finish in 1964; sunburst and natural became available a year later. The natural finish is on the top only; the back and sides are walnut stain—an unusual finish combination for an archtop guitar. Gruhn Guitars/DL

◀ *Electro II 6192-3, 1952.*
See pages 90 and 91.

FULL-DEPTH HOLLOWBODIES
▼ ▼ ▼

Gretsch

The Fred Gretsch Co. of Brooklyn, New York, was a full-line instrument distributor as well as a manufacturer. Founded in 1883, Gretsch achieved notoriety as a banjo and drum maker in the 1920s and made a successful transition to archtop guitars in the 1930s, gaining a reputation for large, fancy models with cat's-eye soundholes. Unlike virtually all other guitar manufacturers in the years prior to World War II, Gretsch refused to explore the sound of the electric guitar. Its prewar electric guitar line consisted of a single plain model that was not even introduced until 1940.

After World War II, Gretsch maintained its faith in acoustic archtops and continued to refine its fancy Synchromatic line. The company's philosophy changed abruptly in 1951, however, with the publication of a catalog featuring downgraded acoustic archtops (no more cat's-eye soundholes or gold sparkle bindings) and three new electric archtops. The new models were developed and brought to market so fast they did not even have their own names. One still bore the acoustic line name—Synchromatic—on the peghead. The 16-inch non-cutaway and the 17-inch cutaway models were both called Electro II (II stood for two pickups); the 16-inch cutaway, available with one or two pickups, was called the Electromatic. The one model already in existence—a 16-inch noncutaway, single-pickup guitar—was dubbed the Electromatic Spanish. (These models were more easily delineated by the four-digit model numbers Gretsch instituted in 1949.)

Gretsch electrics caused a ripple in the early 1950s guitar market. By 1955 Gretsch was ready to make a splash with bold new lines of hollow- and solidbody models. The 1955 Gretsch catalog was titled "Guitars for Moderns," and it set new standards for catalogs as well as guitar designs, although some of the models had already been in production a year or two. Jazz guitarist Jimmie Webster, developer of the fingertapping system later popularized in rock music by Eddie Van Halen, had joined the company by 1953, and his imaginative ideas were beginning to emerge. One of the highlights of the new models was a range of colorful finishes, and, appropriately, the 1955 catalog cover was printed in full color, showing guitars in green, burgundy, black, red, orange, yellow, and white. Gone were the boring variations on the Electro model name; Corvette, Country Club, and Streamliner created a new, dynamic imagery. The only generic model names, such as Hollow Body and Solid Body, were preceded by the name of Nashville guitar star Chet Atkins.

The new guitars—especially the Chet Atkins Hollow Body—gave Gretsch a new identity, and the company never let up in its efforts to improve its guitars. Designs and equipment changed so often that Gretsch aficionados are fond of saying "All Gretsch models are transitional." (Hollowbody models were gradually thinned to a depth of two inches. Although these later versions are not full-depth hollowbodies and should properly be grouped with thinbody guitars, they are included in this section to preserve model continuity.) Through the 1950s, 1960s, and 1970s, through a change in ownership, through the rise of solidbody guitars and the boom in acoustic flat tops during the folk era, Gretsch always based its success on its electric hollowbody guitars.

The Gretsch family sold the company to Baldwin in 1967, and production was moved from Brooklyn to Booneville, Arkansas, in 1970. By 1980 the company had been sold again, and the model changes were so numerous that models no longer resembled their 1950s ancestors of the same name. Booneville production ended in 1981, but some instruments were assembled in Mexico as late as 1984. In early 1985 the Gretsch brand name was acquired by Fred Gretsch, great-grandson of the founder. In 1990 the company introduced Japanese-made models that, though not exact replicas of classic Gretsches, did combine features from various versions of classic models.

▶ *Gretsch Country Club, 1953. Model 6192 was named Country Club in 1953 and offered with a Cadillac green finish (model 6196). New features include the "T-roof" peghead logo, Melita adjustable-saddle bridge, "G" tailpiece, and a pickup selector switch (not visible in this photo) on the upper bass bout. Some plastic materials used in pickguards and bindings from the 1930s through the 1950s tend to deteriorate, as seen in this example. This guitar still has its original case, bank loan agreement marked "Paid," and lifetime guarantee against defective workmanship and materials. With the guarantee the 1955 catalog says, "You can't lose when you invest in a Gretsch Guitar." In this case the catalog was right. This model listed for $395 and is worth considerably more than that now. Crawford White/WC*

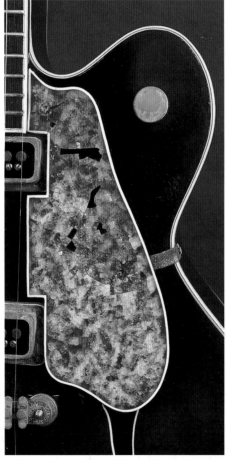

◀ Gretsch Country Club with Project-o-sonic stereo, 1958. The year 1958 brought more changes to the Country Club (and most other high-end Gretsch models), including a roller bridge, "thumb-print" fingerboard inlays, and double-coil "Filter 'Tron" pickups. In addition, Gretsch offered optional stereo wiring (model 6101). This first version of Project-o-sonic stereo uses what are best described as half-pick-ups (above). The neck pickup has poles only for the bass strings, and that signal is fed into one channel. The other channel carries the signal from the bridge pickup, which has poles only for the treble strings. A different system, introduced in 1959 on the White Falcon and adopted by the Country Club in 1960, employs two full pickups that can be split, three three-position tone selectors, and a three-posi-tion pickup selector to achieve, according to catalog claims, 54 different "color variations." Gruhn Guitars/DL

◀ Gretsch Country Club, 1957. The Country Club continued to change with a gold plastic pickguard in 1954 and "humptop block" fingerboard inlays in 1955. Gruhn Guitars/DL

93

▲ Gretsch Corvette, 1955. The Corvette, née Electromatic Spanish, was the cheapest electric guitar in the 1955 catalog, but it made the cover with this optional jaguar tan finish (model 6184). The Corvette was discontinued in 1959, but the name was revived later on a solidbody model. John Seymour/WC

▶ Gretsch Streamliner, 1956. Gretsch's 16-inch cutaway electric of 1949 became the Streamliner. It retained the old Electromatic peghead veneer until 1958 when it began changing into the Anniversary model. The bamboo yellow top with copper mist back and sides (model 6189) is one of four optional finishes. Mike Tepee/WC

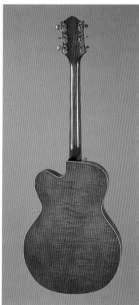

◀ *Gretsch Chet Atkins Hollow Body prototype, 1954. This guitar incorporates ideas from Jimmie Webster and the Gretsch company, among them the Western motif and "amber red" finish, but it does not yet show Atkins's input. A model number had not yet been assigned, so this guitar is labeled "Streamliner Special". The back sports the figured maple of a high-end guitar. Chet Atkins/DL*

▲ Gretsch Chet Atkins Hollow Body, 1959. Like all Gretsch models, the 6120 changed constantly. By 1959 the fingerboard is ebony with thumbprint inlays, a zero fret has been added, the G brand is gone from the top, a horseshoe has replaced the longhorn on the peghead, the "Gretsch by Bigsby" vibrato is a new design, and the pickups are Filter 'Trons. As a result of Atkins's quest for greater sustain, the top braces have been extended all the way to the back so that the guitar is now a semi-solidbody model. John Gillian/BM

▼ Gretsch Chet Atkins Hollow Body (model 6120), 1955. Chet Atkins wanted two features in a guitar: a vibrato and maximum sustaining power. The Bigsby vibrato accomplished the first goal; the metal nut and simple metal bridge helped achieve the second. As for the other features, Atkins later said he did not necessarily care for the Western ornamentation, but he was so glad to have his own model that he would have played just about anything. The "belt buckle" tailpiece of the prototype ended up on a solidbody model, the Round-Up. American Guitar Center/BM

◀ Gretsch Chet Atkins Nashville, 1964. The Chet Atkins Hollow Body was generally known by its model number, 6120, until 1964 when it was dubbed Nashville and given a nameplate on the peghead. By the time the double-cutaway body appeared in mid to late 1961, body depths on Gretsch hollowbodies had been reduced to about two-and-a-quarter inches. In 1963 they would be reduced to two inches. With the move to a double-cutaway body, the Nashville incorporated several features from the more expensive Chet Atkins Country Gentleman: painted-on f-holes and a string mute. Real soundholes were reintroduced in 1973. The backpad appeared just before the change to double-cutaway. Gretsch eventually marketed a total of eight different Atkins models. The three early hollowbodies—6120, Country Gentleman, and Tennessean—were mainstays in the line until Atkins's endorsement agreement ended in 1978. Strings West Tulsa/BM

▶ Gretsch Chet Atkins Country Gentleman, 1958. Following the initial success of the Chet Atkins Hollow Body, Gretsch introduced a larger 17-inch model, the Chet Atkins Country Gentleman (model 6122), in late 1957. The f-holes are closed (they were opened in 1972), the tuners are fancier, and the finish is darker, but otherwise this is very similar to the 16-inch model 6120. Jim Colclasure/DL

▼ Gretsch Chet Atkins Country Gentleman, 1962. By 1962 the Country Gentleman has a double-cutaway body, a standby switch on the lower treble bout, and a double mute system. Two large screw knobs located on either side of the bridge raise and lower the mutes. Levers replaced the screw system in early 1963. After Atkins left Gretsch, this model continued as the Southern Belle. Atkins took the Country Gentleman and the Tennessean model names with him, and they appeared in the Gibson line in 1987 and 1990, respectively. Jacksonville Guitars/SE

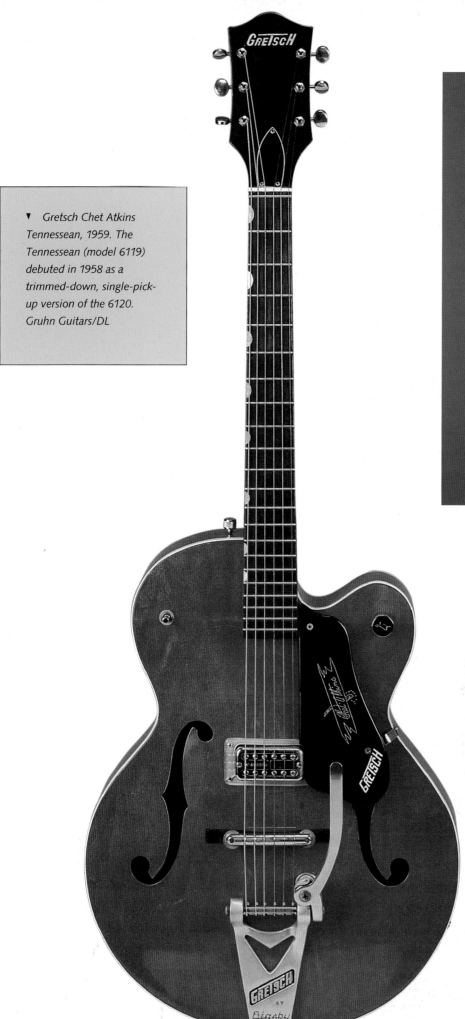

▼ *Gretsch Chet Atkins Tennessean, 1959. The Tennessean (model 6119) debuted in 1958 as a trimmed-down, single-pick-up version of the 6120. Gruhn Guitars/DL*

▲ *Gretsch Chet Atkins Tennessean, 1964. By the time this guitar was made, the Tennessean had become significantly different from the other two Atkins hollow-bodies. Like other low-end models, the Tennessean never changed to a double-cutaway body. It has two pickups, but these are Gretsch's low-end-style Hi-Lo 'Trons rather than the Filter 'Tron of the early Tennessean and the higher models. Jacksonville Guitars/SE*

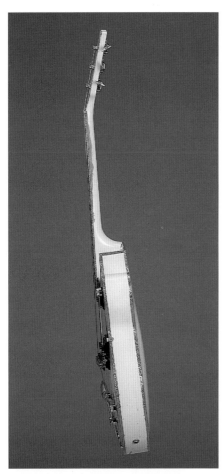

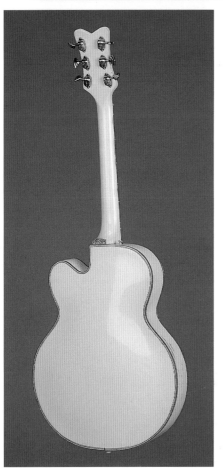

◀ Gretsch White Falcon, 1955. "Cost was never considered in the planning of this guitar," says the 1955 catalog that introduced the White Falcon (model 6136). The Falcon's list price of $600 was $200 higher than the next most expensive electric, the natural-finish Country Club. Falcon and bird motifs include the wings engraved into the fingerboard inlay, a falcon on the pickguard, and gold wings on the peghead. The side binding is a gold sparkle material. (The earliest examples have gold leaf paint under clear plastic binding.) Collectors refer to the special tailpiece as the "Cadillac" style because of the V shape's similarity to a Cadillac hood ornament. A red rhinestone acts as a position marker on the control knobs. Joe Lacy/DL

▲ Gretsch White Falcon, 1966. The changes continue with a horizontal peghead logo (1958), double-cutaway body (1962), and string mutes (1962). The vibrato tailpiece with adjustable arm is unique among Gretsch models but hardly as elegant as the earlier Cadillac style. The offset dot inlay on the fingerboard shows another Gretsch innovation—the "tempered" fingerboard with slanted frets in the upper "T-zone" area developed in 1964 to compensate for intonation problems. Gruhn Guitars/BM

▶ Gretsch White Falcon and Electromatic Twin amplifier, 1958. Even the high-flying White Falcon could not escape such across-the-line changes as thumbprint fingerboard inlay and roller bridge. This guitar still has its original strap, hang tags, case, and case cover. Jay Levin/BM

◀ Gretsch White Falcon, 1979 (far left). Collectors today value single-cutaway Gretsch models over their later double-cutaway namesakes, and apparently the same preference was shown by White Falcon customers in the early 1970s. A single-cutaway Falcon reappeared in the early 1970s, but it is too different from the original versions to be considered a reissue. Bo McDonald/BM

◀ Gretsch Convertible, 1956 (near left). The Convertible, introduced in 1955, reflects the preference of jazz players for a guitar whose acoustic qualities are not compromised by the addition of electronics. Gretsch started with an acoustic guitar body, as documented by a label inside this guitar bearing an acoustic Synchromatic model number (6030) and a 1953 serial number. That label was scratched through with a pencil, probably when a second label was added, bearing the Convertible's model number: 6199. Although the controls are mounted in the pickguard, the pickup is not floating off the top but screwed down. The Convertible is the first Gretsch with a two-tone finish: lotus ivory top and copper mist back and sides (left). Sunburst was available by special order only. Gruhn Guitars/WC

▶ *Gretsch Double Anniversary, 1964 (far right). Gretsch celebrated its 75th anniversary in 1958 with a new model, available with one or two pickups. It inaugurated yet another Gretsch color, two-tone smoke green, and also came with a standard sunburst finish. Early examples have Filter 'Tron pickups; Hi-Lo 'Trons appeared in 1961. From 1961 to 1963 the Double Anniversary was also available with stereo wiring that combines the "half-pickup" system of the early Country Club stereo models with the weaker Hi-Lo (lower right) 'Trons. Gruhn Guitars/DL*

▼ *Gretsch Sal Salvador, 1963. Sal Salvador posed in Gretsch ads with a Convertible in 1958. That same year he was given his own model—sort of. The Sal Salvador model is really a revamped Convertible with a Filter 'Tron pickup, a zero fret and sunburst finish as standard. In 1965 the controls were moved from the pickguard to the top, and the model lasted only two more years. The Bigsby vibrato has been added. Gruhn Guitars/WC*

▼ Gretsch custom, labeled 6117, 1964. Cat's-eye soundholes identified Gretsch's high-end Synchromatic acoustic archtops, but they never appeared on any standard electric model. It is surprising to find them on a guitar with the low-end Hi-Lo 'Tron pickups. The label on this guitar says it is a model 6117, a sunburst Double Anniversary, and so it is in all respects but the finish and the soundholes. Two hundred of these guitars were made from 1964 to 1967, and some of them have a black finish. Half were sent to Manny's, a New York dealer, and half went to a West Coast dealer. Gruhn Guitars/WC

▲ Gretsch Anniversary, 1964. In 1964 the Anniversary was offered with a two-tone tan finish (above left). Unlike almost all other Gretsch finishes, the two-tone tan Anniversary does not have its own model number but shares 6125 with the smoke green Anniversary. Gruhn Guitars/WC

105

▶ Gretsch Sam Goody, 1967. Many dealers throughout the history of American guitars have ordered special limited runs of instruments. Sam Goody, a New York retailer, ordered this model with G-shaped soundholes. Gruhn Guitars/WC

▲ Gretsch Monkees, 1968. The Monkees, a made-for-TV pop music group, were so popular that Gretsch developed a Monkees guitar. The only Gretsch with double-thumbprint inlay, it lasted about as long as the group, from 1966 to 1969. Rod Norwood/BM

▼ Gretsch Viking, 1968. The Viking, introduced in 1964, was the first Gretsch model to debut as a double-cutaway. With it Gretsch introduced the T-zone fingerboard, Super 'Tron pickups, and "tuning fork" bridge. The bridge, which in 1966 made its way onto the White Falcon, Black Hawk, and Van Eps models, is a floating type. An A-440 tuning fork extends through the body, supposedly to improve resonance. This bridge made accurate intonation impossible, and most players removed it and slid the roller bridge forward over the hole. Perhaps the Viking's best quality was its availability in Cadillac green as well as sunburst and natural. It lasted until 1975. Music Studio/BM

◀ *Rickenbacker SP, late 1940s. Rickenbacker emerged from World War II in 1946 with unshaken faith in Hawaiian guitars. The lone standard guitar, the Spanish or SP, had a Rickenbacker pickup and peghead plate, but the body and neck were made by Harmony. The model lasted only until 1950. After the SP just one full-depth model (and it was not as deep as a typical Gibson full-depth) was ever put into production: the double-cut-away 381, best known as the model played by John Kay of Steppenwolf. Edward Fest/BM*

FULL-DEPTH HOLLOWBODIES
▼ ▼ ´▼

Other Makers

After Gibson, Epiphone, and Gretsch, Guild was the only maker of full-depth hollowbody electrics to gain widespread respect from players in the postwar years. Significantly, Guild's initial workforce was made up largely of former Epiphone employees. National, a pioneering company in the electric market, was never more than an also-ran in the archtop electric field after World War II. Martin, the oldest and most respected maker of acoustic flat top guitars, made only token efforts to market electric instruments. Rickenbacker, the company that started the electric business, had little success with full-depth hollowbody guitars but a great deal of success with thinbody models. Fender, which revolutionized the industry with solidbody electrics, launched its first attack on the hollowbody market with a thinbody design; later full-depth Fenders were expensive but unsuccessful.

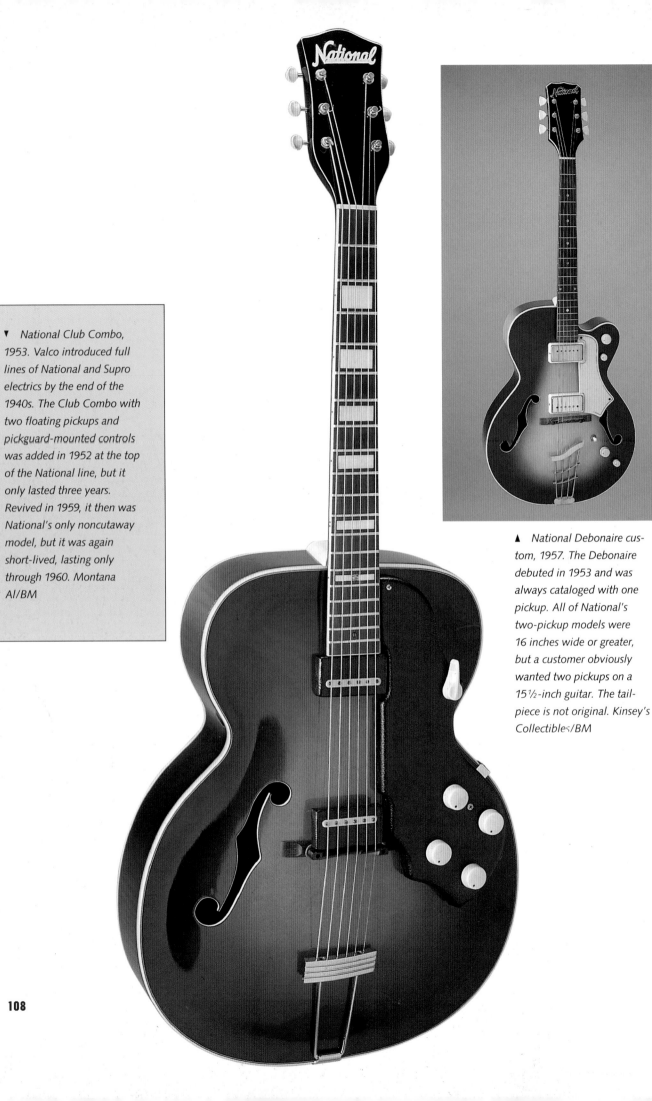

▼ *National Club Combo, 1953. Valco introduced full lines of National and Supro electrics by the end of the 1940s. The Club Combo with two floating pickups and pickguard-mounted controls was added in 1952 at the top of the National line, but it only lasted three years. Revived in 1959, it then was National's only noncutaway model, but it was again short-lived, lasting only through 1960. Montana AI/BM*

▲ *National Debonaire custom, 1957. The Debonaire debuted in 1953 and was always cataloged with one pickup. All of National's two-pickup models were 16 inches wide or greater, but a customer obviously wanted two pickups on a 15½-inch guitar. The tailpiece is not original. Kinsey's Collectibles/BM*

◀ *National Bel-Aire, 1958.*
The body of National's new
model of 1953, the Bel-Aire,
not only looks like a Gibson
ES-175, it is an ES-175 body,
supplied by Gibson. This
example even has a Gibson
factory-order number
stamped inside. Gibson was
probably so accommodating
to its competitor because
Gibson's parent company,
C. M. I., also distributed
Valco instruments during this
period. Kinsey's Collect-
ibles/BM

▼ *National Bel-Aire, 1960.*
In a last-ditch attempt to
save its full-depth hollow-
bodies, National upgraded
the Bel-Aire with a third
pickup and fancier ornamen-
tation in 1958. Buyers did
not respond, and National
discontinued all full-depth
electrics in 1961. In addition
to the Gibson-made body,
this guitar has been further
Gibsonized with a Gibson
bridge and tailpiece. Clifford
Antone/BM

▼ *Guild Stratford 375, 1955. Guild was founded in New York in 1952 by musician and music store owner Alfred Dronge. Many of Guild's early employees came from the failing Epiphone company, and, not surprisingly, Dronge's company quickly gained a reputation for high-quality archtop guitars. The most obvious descendant of the Epiphone tradition is the Stratford 350: a 17-inch version of Epi's 18-inch Emperor. Emperor characteristics include the three pickups and push-button selector system. The harp tailpiece is a Guild trademark. In Guild's 1954 catalog the natural-finish X-350 was designated X-375 (X denotes an electric model in Guild nomenclature). Although future catalogs used "X-350" for both finishes, instrument labels retained the distinction for several years. Gruhn Guitars/WC*

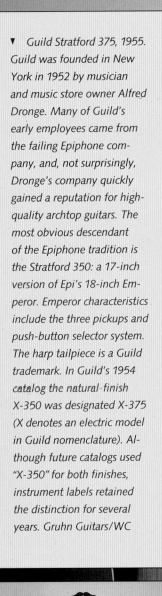

◀ *Guild Stuart 500, 1956. The Stuart 500 is the same size as the Stratford 350 but with two rather than three pickups. Nevertheless, its ornamentation—particularly the Epiphone-style mother-of-pearl inlay with abalone pearl wedges—makes it Guild's top electric model. The five-piece neck construction is another Epiphone characteristic. Johnny Smith's identification with this model helped Guild gain acceptance among jazz players. Ironically, when Smith was given his own model, it was not an electric model but an acoustic, a fancier version of the A-500, with a floating pickup. The Melita bridge on this example is not original. On Stage Music/DL*

▶ *Guild X-550, 1955. Like the X-350/X-375, the X-500 with natural finish was referred to as model X-550 in the 1954 catalog and on later instrument labels. Guild's higher models are easily identifiable by their G peghead logo. Like Epiphone, Gibson, and other makers of fine archtop guitars, Guild chose the curliest maple for the backs of high-end models. Gruhn Guitars/WC*

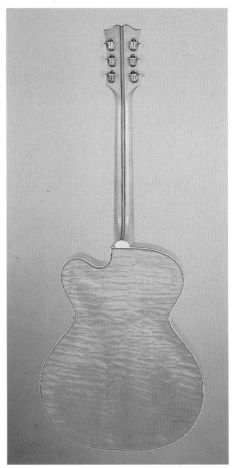

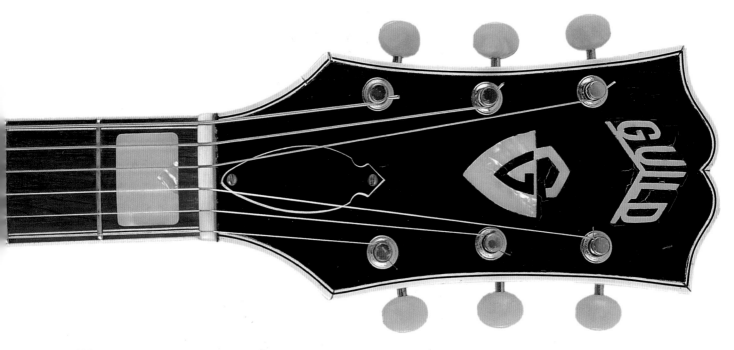

▲ Fender LTD, 1971. Roger Rossmeisl, the German-born designer responsible for Rickenbacker's most successful models, was hired by Fender in 1962 to design acoustic flat tops. In 1969 Fender introduced two Rossmeisl-designed full-depth hollow-body electrics, the fancier being the LTD. The LTD has many features not found previously on a Fender, including the floating pickup, inlay patterns, and peghead design. The neck, however, is attached like that of all other Fenders of this period—with four bolts (above center). As its name implies, the LTD was produced in limited quantities. It was discontinued by 1976 after only 75 instruments were made. John Brinkman/DL

▼ Martin D-28E, 1959. About 25 years after all the other major guitar manufacturers had introduced electric guitars, the venerable Martin company took notice. Martin's idea of an electric guitar was simply a standard acoustic guitar with a DeArmond pickup or two, and electric versions of the 00-18, D-18, and D-28 debuted in 1959. Similar pickups had just been phased out at Gretsch, and most makers were moving to double-coil humbucking pickups on high-end models. With outdated electronics and a questionable market for electric flat tops—especially those with diminished acoustic properties—the Martins were doomed. The D-18E died the same year it appeared; the D-28E and the 00-18E held on into 1964. Joseph Nuyens/DL

▶ Ampeg Baby Bass, late 1960s. The Ampeg company name came from an amplified sound post or peg in an acoustic bass, a system developed by New York bassist Everett Hull in 1947. The company made amplifiers exclusively until the debut of the Baby Bass in 1962. Unlike the most popular electric bass, the Fender Precision, which has frets and is played like a guitar, the Ampeg model has the look (albeit reduced) and feel of an upright acoustic bass. The most popular Baby Bass color is a traditional sunburst, but a few were made in bright red and other colors. Gruhn Guitars/WC

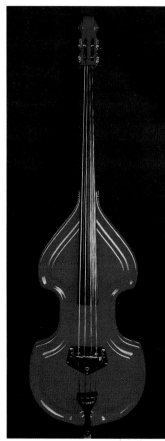

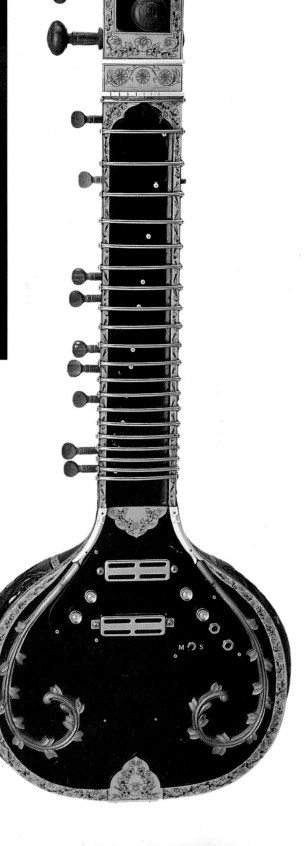

▶ Rajah Zeetar, late 1960s. The Rajah Zeetar may have been closer to a true electrified sitar than were the Danelectro and Coral sitars (see page 192), but that did not make it a success. Pete Ramirez/BM

114

SOLIDBODIES

▼ ▼ ▼

Fender

Leo Fender was by no means the first to build a solidbody electric guitar, but he was the first to make it a commercial success. Rickenbacker's Bakelite model of the mid 1930s had serious drawbacks, including the short scale length of a lap steel (to go with its lap steel appearance), molded frets, and tuning problems caused by Bakelite's sensitivity to temperature changes. Slingerland's

model of the late 1930s was mentioned in the catalog (with no accompanying illustration) as a Spanish-neck variation of a lap steel model rather than as a revolutionary new style of guitar. Les Paul, who would later endorse Gibson's most successful line of solidbodies, had proved by 1940 that the solidbody concept was viable with his homemade "Log," but no manufacturer picked up his design. Paul Bigsby, who is best known for a vibrato design, made several custom-ordered solidbody guitars but never attempted to be a full-time guitar manufacturer.

The Fender company was a fledgling manufacturer of lap steels and amplifiers when its representatives arrived at the National Association of Music Merchants trade show in 1950 with the new Esquire Spanish-neck guitar. Like Fender's lap steels, it was a no-frills instrument. The body was a slab of ash with a single cutaway. The neck and fingerboard were made of a single piece of maple with no truss rod, and it was attached to the body by four large screws. Next to conventional electric guitars, with their carved tops and dovetail neck joints, the Fender Esquire must have looked like a high school wood shop project. Anyone with access to a band saw could duplicate the body; anyone with the ability to turn a screwdriver could set the neck. A single-pickup guitar was anything but impressive in 1950, the year after Gibson had introduced its fancy three-pickup ES-5. And the finish—in a time of rich, honey-shaded sunbursts and stunning natural finishes—was "blonde," a pale wash that let some of the wood grain show through.

In the wider context of furniture and graphic design of the 1950s, the bold simplicity of the Esquire may have been on the cutting edge of American modernism, but the guitar-playing public probably did not view it that way. Certainly, dealers and manufacturers thought it had little chance of success, especially considering that up until then Fender had made only steel guitars and amps. Then again, few in the instrument industry would have looked at the early home-baked K&F lap steels of 1946 and predicted any future at all for Leo Fender.

After a rocky start in late 1950 Fender's single-pickup Esquire and double-pickup Telecaster (née Broadcaster) began to find a market, and in 1951 the company introduced an even more radical and revolutionary instrument: the solidbody Precision electric bass. With Fender showing signs of success, other manufacturers reacted quickly. Gibson unveiled the Les Paul Model solidbody in mid-1952, National introduced several cheaply made solidbody models the same year, and Gretsch got in the market by mid-1953. Fender surged ahead again in 1954 with the Stratocaster, which refined the original 1950 solidbody design.

Leo Fender continued to refine and improve the concept of the solidbody guitar (although many players believe he reached the pinnacle of design with the Stratocaster) until he sold his company to CBS Records in 1965. Under CBS, the Fender electric line was expanded with semi-hollow and hollowbody models, but the quality of Fender products began to decline. By the early 1970s the company refocused on its proven solidbody models, and various spinoffs and vintage reissues of the old standbys—the Telecaster, Stratocaster, and Precision—were introduced. In the early 1980s CBS developed a Japanese-made line—again led by the Telecaster, Stratocaster, and Precision—which was marketed domestically under the Squier name.

CBS sold Fender in 1985 to a group led by Bill Schultz, and the company continues to be a leading maker of solidbody electrics. Various reissues and "signature" (artist endorsement) variations of classic models are among the most popular instruments on the market. In addition, so many makers have copied Fender's basic Stratocaster design that it has become an icon for the electric guitar.

Leo Fender stayed in retirement only a few months before hiring on as a consultant to CBS. He then formed CLF Research, later joined by his longtime associate George Fullerton. Two other former Fender associates, Forrest White and Tom Walker, joined Fender to form Music Man in 1972 and granted CLF Research the exclusive contract to build Music Man instruments.

In 1979 Dale Hyatt of the Randall company, George Fullerton, and Leo Fender formed G&L. G&L's most popular models represent Fender's further development of the Telecaster and Stratocaster concepts. Leo Fender died March 21, 1991.

◀ *Fender prototype, 1949. Although Leo Fender rented out his 1943 prototype to musicians, this 1949 guitar was the first one built to be a player's instrument. It sports the cutaway body shape, slant-mounted pickup, and one-piece neck (bolted to the body) that would become the Esquire—the model that would make history in the electric guitar world. The pickup cover slides onto the bridge plate. John Hanley/WC*

Fender MUSICAL INSTRUMENTS / 500 S. RAYMOND, FULLERTON, CALIF. / 526-6624
a division of Columbia Records Distribution Corp.

February 23, 1965

Mr. Roy Acuff

Dear Roy:

Thought perhaps I should supply you with a little information regarding the Fender Guitar I am sending you for the museum.

The Guitar was made in 1943, the first, primarily it was designed and developed for the patents applied for on the pickup assembly. This same pickup assembly was used on all of our steel guitars until approximately 1956. The instrument is all handmade of oakwood.

It might be interesting to note, the guitar was rented out to various entertainers for their engagements, requiring a two week advance notice, it remained in constant use on this basis until 1950.

We did not attempt to clean it up in any way as this would spoil the authenticity of the instrument.

Very truly yours,

C. L. Fender

C. L. Fender

CLF:do

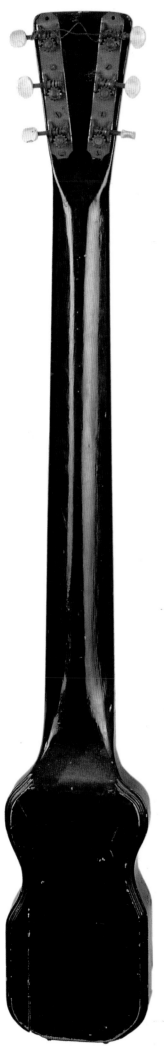

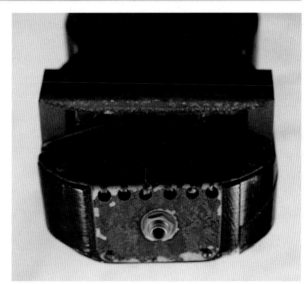

◀ *Fender prototype, 1943. Leo Fender's letter to Roy Acuff identifies this guitar as a prototype, built three years before the first K&F instrument. The pickup is Fender's unique design with the strings passing through the coil of magnet wire. The roller-type controls would not appear on a Fender model until the Jazzmaster of 1958. The jack is at the end of the body, where it would be on K&F and early Fender lap steels, but the round neck shows that this is a standard guitar. Although Fender's first production guitars were still seven years away, the genesis of the Fender legacy is apparent in this instrument's round neck and guitar-shaped body. Roy Acuff Museum, Opryland USA/WC*

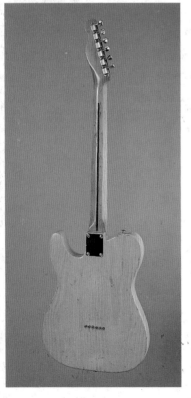

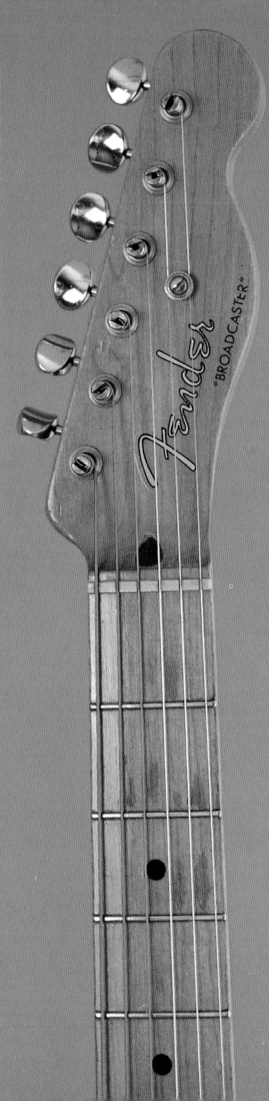

▼ *Fender Broadcaster, 1950 (facing page, top left). The 1950 Esquire had no truss rod, and neck warpage was a serious problem. Late in the year Fender stopped Esquire production temporarily and introduced the Broadcaster, a two-pickup version of the Esquire with a truss rod. The dark "skunk stripe" (facing page, lower left) and the wood plug in the peghead (right) show where the neck was routed for truss rod installation. The controls (left) appear to be the same as those of today's Telecaster—volume, tone, and pickup selector—but in the early years the "tone" knob is actually a pickup mixer control, and the switch works as both a tone selector (for the neck pickup) and a straight pickup selector. Gruhn Guitars/WC*

▲ *Fender Telecaster, 1953. In April 1951 the nameless Fender model was christened Telecaster. Like the original name, Broadcaster, the new name related to the newest technological advances. The wiring was changed in 1952 to provide a true tone control, but the dual-pickup switch setting was lost in the process and would not be available on the Telecaster until 1967. Toby Ruckert/WC*

▲ Fender "No-caster," 1951. Gretsch had been using the Broadkaster name on drums and guitars since the 1930s, so Fender had to find something new. For a short time "Broadcaster" was snipped off the peghead decal (right), and these guitars have since been dubbed "No-casters" by collectors. The form-fit case has a bulbous area around the peghead, earning it the nickname "thermometer" case. Gary Bohannon/WC

▲ Fender Telecaster, 1955. In late 1954 the Telecaster's black Bakelite pickguard was replaced with white plastic. The finish has become lighter and closer to a blond shade than the transparent butterscotch finish of earlier blackguard examples. Clifford Antone/BM

◀ *Fender Telecaster custom left-handed, 1952. Many Telecasters in the late 1960s and 1970s have a Bigsby vibrato specially designed for the low bridge of a solidbody guitar. In the early 1950s, however, Bigsbys were only made to fit archtops, and this example shows a solidbody vibrato design in progress. The elevated bridge moves the strings too far away from the pickup; a spacer raises the pickup to the proper distance. Gruhn Guitars/WC*

▼ *Fender Telecaster, 1953. The hinges on the "thermometer" cases did not line up properly, and Fender quickly designed a new case with one straight side. Clifford Antone/BM*

▼ Fender Esquire, 1963. The Esquire went through the same changes as the Telecaster. The only difference was in popularity. Although the Telecaster was overshadowed by the Stratocaster and later the Jazzmaster and Jaguar, its basic simplicity and functionality secured it a solid place in the Fender line. The Esquire, possibly because of its single pickup (even though few players ever use the neck pickup of a Telecaster), faded into obscurity, and the last were made in early 1970. Gary Bohannon/BM

▲ Fender Telecaster, 1960, with Bassman amp, 1959. The Telecaster underwent many minor changes between 1954 and 1959, including the string guide, position of the logo decal, shape of the selector switch cap, and bridge design (with strings loading through the bridge rather than through the body). The most obvious change came in late 1959, when the one-piece maple neck-fingerboard was replaced by a maple neck with a separate rosewood fingerboard. Although the Bassman amp was designed for the Precision bass, the late-1950s version is considered by many to be one of the greatest guitar amps ever made. Gary Bohannon/DL

◀ Fender Telecaster Wild-
wood Thinline prototype,
1966 (far left). This guitar
appears to be a prototype
gone astray. A similar semi-
hollow body would be introduced in 1968 on the Telecaster Thinline to provide a
lighter instrument. But no
production Telecaster variation ever had green-grained
wood, backward f-holes, or
a Jazzmaster neck. "Wild-
wood" (basswood injected
with a chemical to cause the
color change) (near left) was
used on acoustic flat-top guitars and on Coronado thinbody electrics in the 1960s.
Longtime Fender employee
Bill Carson speculates that
this guitar represents one
employee's suggestion for
using up surplus Wildwood.
Gruhn Guitars/WC

◀ Fender Esquire Custom,
1959. By 1959 the Esquire
and Telecaster were posi-
tioned in the middle of the
Fender line, below the
Stratocaster and Jazzmaster,
above the short-scale Duo-
Sonic and Musicmaster. The
soundness of the Tele design
led to numerous offshoot
models, led by the Telecaster
Custom and Esquire Custom
in mid 1959. The Customs
are more highly ornamented,
with a bound body and
sunburst finish, but are
otherwise the same as the
standard models. Rod
Norwood/WC

125

▲ Fender Telecaster Thinline, 1968. The Telecaster Thinline was put into production in late 1968. Only the bass side of the body, with the f-hole, is hollow. The Thinline was initially offered in ash, like this example, or rosewood, with custom colors available. In a rare break with Fender tradition, the peghead does not bear the full model name. In 1972 the model was fitted with two humbucking pickups, and "Telecaster Thinline" was added to the peghead decal. It was discontinued in 1979. Joe Hardman/DL

▶ Fender Telecaster prototype, 1983. This fancy Telecaster, with three-piece walnut and maple body, gold-plated metal parts, and vibrato, was never put into production. Bill Carson/DL

▲ Fender Custom Telecaster, 1974. A second Custom version of the Telecaster, with "Custom" preceding "Telecaster," appeared in 1970. The bridge pickup is standard Tele style, but the neck pickup is a double-coil humbucker that probably represents a belated response to Gibson's success with humbuckers. The Gibson influence is obvious from the control configuration: separate volume and tone control for each pickup; selector switch on the upper bass bout. The Custom Telecaster was discontinued in 1981. Jacksonville Guitars/SE

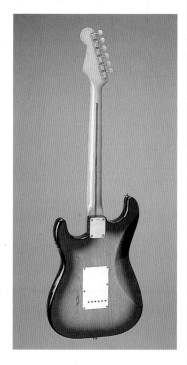

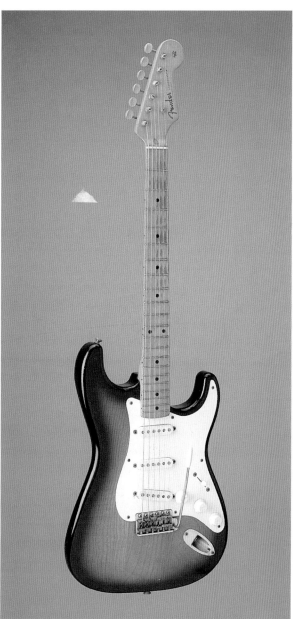

◀ Fender Stratocaster, 1954. Unlike most manufacturers, Leo Fender stuck to his philosophy of leaving successful models alone. Rather than radically revamping the Telecaster, Fender introduced his new ideas in 1954 on a new model: the Stratocaster. In addition to a third pickup, the most notable differences between the Strat and Tele are the double-cutaway body shape, contoured back, and spring-loaded vibrato system. Standard finish on the original Stratocaster is two-tone sunburst. Like the Telecaster of the same period, the Stratocaster case is form-fitting on one side with a straight-line hinged side. Oddly, these cases, with peghead to the right, have the opposite design from virtually all other cases for fretted instruments in the history of American instruments, including later Fender cases. The Stratocaster quickly eclipsed the Telecaster and became one of the all-time classic electric guitar models. Clifford Antone/BM

▼ *Fender Stratocasters, right-handed and left-handed, 1958. The original Strat was offered only as a vibrato model—or in Fender's terminology, with "tremelo"—but in early 1955 Fender shipped the first non-trem models. Known to collectors as "hardtails," they are easily identified from the back by their lack of a spring cavity and coverplate. The first major change in the Stratocaster, in mid 1958, was cosmetic—a third tone, red, was added to the sunburst finish. The left-handed example is missing the vibrato arm. Scott Jennings/BM*

▼ *Fender Stratocaster, 1963, with Vibroverb amplifier. The move to rosewood fingerboards in 1959 extended across the entire Fender line. The only other obvious change is the three-layer laminated pickguard which replaced the single-ply style in 1959. Jimmy Wallace/DL*

▲ *Fender Stratocaster, 1964. This one-of-a-kind Lucite Strat was built so that the Fender sales staff could see every part of the instrument. John Sprung/ John Peden*

◀ Fender Duo-Sonic, 1958. Fender courted the low-end market in mid 1956 with two budget models: the two-pickup Duo-Sonic and the single-pickup Musicmaster. The anodized aluminum pickguard is standard equipment on these models and the Jazzmaster during this period. Clifford Antone/BM

▼ Fender Jazzmaster, 1959. As the Strat had been the vehicle for new ideas in 1954, so the Jazzmaster was in mid 1958. Innovations include offset body waists, new-style pickups, preset tone capabilities, and "floating tremelo" (not anchored by springs on the back of the body). Despite its place in the line as a higher model than the Stratocaster, the Jazzmaster was never as widely accepted as the Strat and was discontinued in 1981. This example sports a custom-ordered blond finish. Gil Southworth/BM

▲ Fender Jazzmaster, 1968. In the mid-1960s, Fender upgraded the ornamentation on high-end models. Finger-board binding was added in late 1965; large block inlays appeared in mid 1966. When maple fingerboards were reintroduced in 1967, some examples featured contrasting black binding and inlays. Jim Colclasure/BM

◄ Fender Jaguar, 1963. Yet another "improved" model, the Jaguar, was introduced in mid 1962. Aside from the obvious differences in pick-ups and electronics, the primary difference between the Jaguar and Jazzmaster is the scale length: 24 inches for the Jaguar, 25½ for the Jazz-master (the same as the Strat and Tele). The Jaguar was discontinued in 1974. This example represents the high end of Fender's high end. In addition to being the most expensive model in the Fender catalog, this guitar was custom ordered with blond finish and gold-plated hardware. Gil Southworth/BM

▲ Fender Electric XII, 1965. Fender's attempt to exploit the folk music boom in its solidbody line produced this 12-string model, introduced in mid 1965. Like other high-end Fenders, it soon received fingerboard binding and block inlays. It was relatively unsuccessful and was discontinued in 1969. Rod Norwood/BM

◄ Fender Swinger, circa 1969. Also known as the Musiclander and Arrow, the Swinger was designed to use up overstocked parts, including Musicmaster electronics and necks (recut) from the low-end Mustang. A fancier "parts" model, the Custom or Maverick, also appeared during the same period, from mid 1969 to 1971. Dave Crocker/BM

► Fender Electric Violin, circa 1956. Fender's first attempt at an electric violin sports such typical Fender features as a solid body, Tele-blond finish, and peghead with all tuners on one side. The slotted peghead is unusual, as are the exaggerated body waists and concealed pickup. The model was put into production briefly in 1958. It reappeared with a more traditional scrolled peghead and ebony tuning pegs from 1969 to 1975. James Eddy Campbell/WC

▼ Fender Mandolin, 1957. Fender's electric mandolin is distinguished from most others by its solidbody construction and four strings (rather than eight). It was introduced in early 1956 with a "slab" body like the Tele; by 1959 the body was contoured like the Strat. Available in sunburst or blond, it lasted until 1976. Garrett/BM

SOLIDBODIES

▼ ▼ ▼

Fender Basses

Just as Fender's Esquire was not the first electric solidbody guitar, Fender's Precision bass of 1951 was not the first electric bass. Gibson acoustical engineer Lloyd Loar made a prototype electric bass in the 1920s, Rickenbacker offered a model in the 1930s, and Ampeg founder Everett Hull developed an amplification system for upright acoustic bass in 1947. Loar probably used

some sort of microphonic pickup; Rickenbacker's bass had a horseshoe pickup similar to its guitar pickups; and Hull picked up a signal from a sound post inside the body of an acoustic bass. All three styles kept the scale length, unfretted fingerboard, and upright playing position of a standard acoustic bass.

Nor was Fender the first with a fretted bass instrument. Gibson had made bass mandolins in the 1910s and 1920s and even a huge bass banjo around 1930. In addition, a large six-string bass guitar, the *bajo sexto* or *guitarron*, was already common in Mexican mariachi bands.

But the Precision bass was something different altogether. Although it had the four strings of a true bass instrument, in other respects it was more like a guitar, with a 34-inch scale (compared with 42 inches on a standard three-quarter-size upright bass), frets, and a solid wood body with a unique double-cutaway guitar shape. Furthermore, the Precision was held and played like a guitar (many electric bassists use a pick). It had the same advantage over an acoustic bass—greater volume—that the electric guitar had over an acoustic, and its guitarlike qualities made it easier for musicians to switch from guitar to bass. Its sound was different from an upright bass—many acoustic bassists compared it to a rubber band—or any other acoustic instrument.

As important as the early Fender guitars are in the history of fretted electric instruments, their impact is dwarfed by the Precision's influence. The Precision not only created a market for electric basses, it dominated its field for more than 30 years like no guitar model ever has.

Unlike the Telecaster, which remained basically the same while new designs led to new models, the Precision was radically revamped in the 1950s, and it remained Fender's only bass model until the Jazz bass appeared in 1961. Various other low-end basses, plus a bass version of the Coronado thinbody archtop guitar, joined the line in the 1960s, but the Precision or "P-bass" remained the dominant model until the late 1980s, when the Jazz bass, with its sharper attack and individual pickup volume controls, began to rival the Precision.

◀ Fender Precision bass, 1959. A new pickguard of anodized aluminum appeared in mid 1957; it would be replaced by a plastic guard in late 1959. Also in mid 1957 a split-coil pickup and a larger peghead appeared. A three-tone sunburst finish was adopted in mid 1958. Aside from the across-the-line move to a rosewood fingerboard in mid 1959, this example represents the final version of the Precision bass. Clifford Antone/BM

◀ Fender Precision bass, early 1957. The P-bass was remodeled with a sunburst finish, white pickguard, and contoured back (above) in 1954. The pickup remained similar to the Telecaster's bridge pickup. Clifford Antone/BM

▼ *Fender Jazz bass, 1962. Stacked knobs were quickly replaced by a volume control for each pickup and a master tone control (the small knob). To some players, the greater sustain provided by a solid body was not a desirable quality, and Fender Jazz basses from 1960 to 1962 have string mutes (right) for a faster, more acoustic-like decay. Gruhn Guitars/DL*

◄ Fender Jazz bass, 1960. In a general sense, the Jazz bass of 1960 was intended to be the Stratocaster and Jazzmaster of the bass world—a new model to introduce new ideas. Like the Strat, it has one more pickup than its predecessor, and like the Jazzmaster, it has offset body waists. Each pickup has controls in a "stacked" or concentric knob configuration, with tone and volume mounted on the same shaft. The fingerboard is narrower at the nut than the Precision's. This example is finished in a custom color: shoreline gold. Jim Colclasure/DL

◄ Fender Bass VI, 1964. Introduced in late 1961, the Bass VI is a true bass guitar. It has a 30-inch scale, which is standard "short-scale" length for electric basses, but its six strings are spaced close together like those of a guitar. It is tuned like a guitar but an octave lower, although many players find a "baritone" tuning, a fourth or a fifth below standard, to be more versatile and effective. Its Jazzmaster-type vibrato should dispel any doubts that it was intended to be a bass. It was not very successful and was discontinued in 1975. Gil Southworth/BM

▶ *Fender Bass V, 1967.
Fender introduced a five-
string bass in mid 1965. The
extra string might have been
appealing to bass players,
but those accustomed to the
Precision sound may well
have been disappointed by
the Bass V's small pickup,
which looks the same as that
of the Electric XII, and its
30-inch scale. Like the high-
end Jazzmaster and Jaguar
guitars, the Jazz, Bass V,
and Bass VI were upgraded
with a bound fingerboard
in late 1965 and block inlays
in mid 1966. Jim Colcla-
sure/BM*

▶ *Fender Telecaster Bass,
1968. In 1982 Fender began
reviving early or classic versions of some models, such
as the '57 Precision ("'57"
is part of the 1982 model
name) or the '62 Precision. In
1968, however, this reissue
of the original P-bass was
named the Telecaster Bass.
The primary differences between the Tele Bass and the
1951 P-bass are the gray
pickup housing and white
pickguard, both of which are
black on the original. In 1972
the Telecaster bass was fitted
with a humbucking pickup. It
was discontinued by 1979.
Jacksonville Guitars/BM*

▲ *Fender bass prototype,
1977. This experimental bass
with a carved top edge
combines a time-proven,
Precision-style pickup and a
double-coil humbucking
pickup. The tuners are at the
bridge, leaving a stubby
peghead that is undoubtedly
offensive to Fender purists.
Gene Fields/BM*

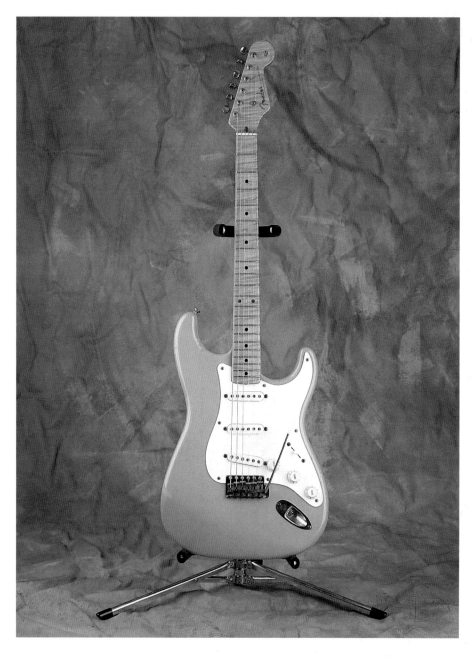

◀ *Fender Stratocaster, 1954. Several decades of aging have left the true color of this guitar impossible to determine. It was probably something close to the "shell pink" of later years. Reeve Little*

SOLIDBODIES

▼ ▼ ▼

Fender Colors

Despite the progressive designs of Fender's mid-1950s guitars, finish choices remained quite conservative: blond for the Telecaster and Esquire, two-tone sunburst for the Stratocaster and Precision bass. By 1961, however, Fender was offering a wide variety of colors.

The roots of Fender's custom colors go back to late 1954, when the company switched from what was probably furniture-grade lacquer to a more

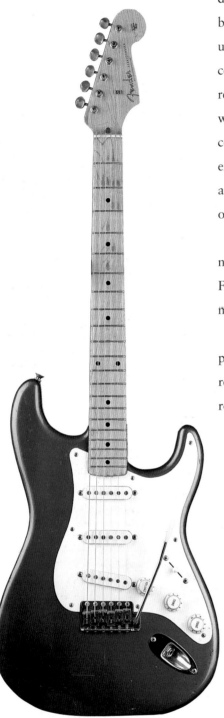

durable automotive grade. The most obvious result was the change in the Tele-blond finish from semitransparent to a creamier, more opaque shade. Fender used DuPont Duco products, so it was no trouble to finish a guitar in any Duco color. Fender did not advertise these custom finishes, but they were available by request. If a catalyst to Fender's move to custom colors can be pinpointed, it would likely have been Gretsch's 1955 "Guitars for Moderns" catalog. Gretsch's colors, however, were identified with specific models. The White Falcon, for example, was white, and although it could conceivably have been ordered in another color, it would not have made much sense. "Cadillac green" belonged on a Country Club; an orange finish belonged on a Chet Atkins Hollow Body.

Fender's approach was the opposite of Gretsch's. When Fender announced the availability of custom colors in 1957, no specific colors were listed. For a 5 percent surcharge, any Duco color was available on any of the high-end models.

In 1961 Fender inaugurated its classic period of custom colors with the publication of a brochure containing 14 paint color samples. The color list was revised in 1963. In 1971 the classic period ended when color ranges were narrowed and offered as standard options rather than special finishes.

▶ *Fender "Mary Kaye" Stratocaster, 1957. This "deluxe" Strat, with blond finish and gold-plated metal parts, was listed as a separate catalog model in 1957. Entertainer Mary Kaye (not the cosmetics entrepreneur) is pictured in Fender literature playing this model, and it has come to be identified by her name. Although blond was the standard finish on the Telecaster, it was a custom finish on the Stratocaster. Gil Southworth/BM*

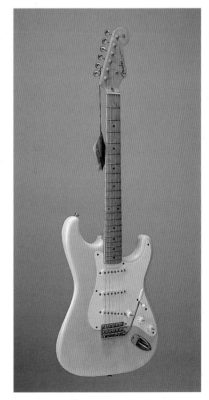

▲ *Fender Stratocaster, turquoise metallic, 1957. Any Duco color was available, and the customer for this guitar ordered a turquoise metallic finish, official name unknown. Reeve Little*

▼ Fender Telecaster, sunburst, 1961. Just as Teleblond was a custom finish on a Strat, sunburst (the standard Strat finish) was a custom color on a Telecaster. Like Strats, sunburst Teles are two-tone prior to mid 1958 and three-tone thereafter. Gordon Dow/BM

▲ Jazzmaster, fiesta red, 1961. Fender employee George Fullerton is credited with standardizing custom finishes in late 1957, and he recalls mixing up the first batch of fiesta red at a local paint store. The first fiesta red instrument was a Jazzmaster, but the color's official debut, on the cover of the 1958–59 catalog, was on a Strat. Gruhn Guitars/DL

◄ Fender Telecaster, red, 1957. Fender had yet to standardize custom colors when this Telecaster was made. Red, blue, gold, white, and black are the custom finishes most often seen in the late 1950s. Clifford Antone/BM

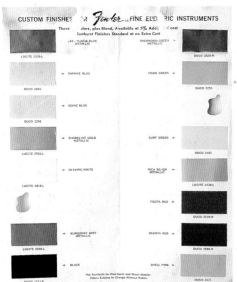

▲ Fender custom color chart, 1961. Enamel lacquers were marketed by DuPont under the Duco brand; acrylic lacquers bore the Lucite brand. Jimmy Wallace/BM

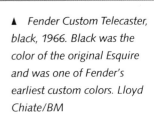

▲ Fender Custom Telecaster, black, 1966. Black was the color of the original Esquire and was one of Fender's earliest custom colors. Lloyd Chiate/BM

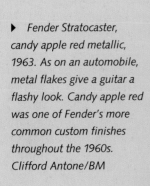

▶ Fender Stratocaster, candy apple red metallic, 1963. As on an automobile, metal flakes give a guitar a flashy look. Candy apple red was one of Fender's more common custom finishes throughout the 1960s. Clifford Antone/BM

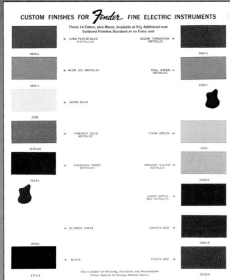

CUSTOM FINISHES FOR *Fender* FINE ELECTRIC INSTRUMENTS

These 14 Colors, plus Blond, Available at 5% Additional cost
Sunburst Finishes Standard at no Extra cost

← LAKE PLACID BLUE METALLIC	OCEAN TURQUOISE METALLIC →
2976-L	4607-L
← BLUE ICE METALLIC	TEAL GREEN METALLIC
4602-L	4297-L
← SONIC BLUE	
2295	
← FIREMIST GOLD METALLIC	FOAM GREEN →
4579-LH	2353
← CHARCOAL FROST METALLIC	FIREMIST SILVER METALLIC
4618-L	4576-H
	CANDY APPLE RED METALLIC →
← OLYMPIC WHITE	DAKOTA RED →
2818-L	2590-H
← BLACK	FIESTA RED →
1711-X	2219-H

Not available for Mustang, Duo-Sonic and Musicmaster
Colors Subject to Change Without Notice

▲ *Fender custom color chart, 1966. Some colors changed in 1963, but the total stayed at 14. Some, such as shoreline gold and Inca silver, changed in name only. Susan Carson/DL*

▶ *Fender Precision, white, 1958 (above right). Depending on the amount of clear lacquer over the finish, white ("Olympic white" after 1961) guitars may age to a deep yellow. Gil Southworth/BM*

▼ *Fender Stratocaster, Lake Placid blue metallic, 1964. Along with candy apple red, Lake Placid blue metallic was a popular 1960s custom color. Rock Video International/BM*

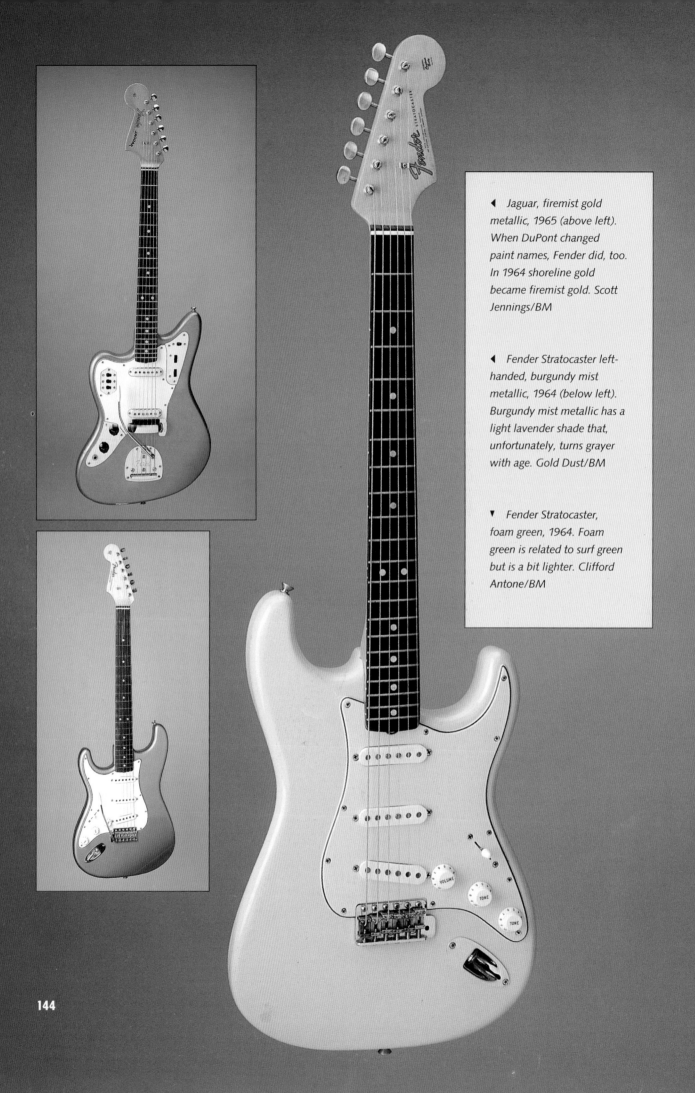

◄ Jaguar, firemist gold metallic, 1965 (above left). When DuPont changed paint names, Fender did, too. In 1964 shoreline gold became firemist gold. Scott Jennings/BM

◄ Fender Stratocaster left-handed, burgundy mist metallic, 1964 (below left). Burgundy mist metallic has a light lavender shade that, unfortunately, turns grayer with age. Gold Dust/BM

▼ Fender Stratocaster, foam green, 1964. Foam green is related to surf green but is a bit lighter. Clifford Antone/BM

◀ *Fender Stratocaster, teal green metallic, 1969. This guitar appears to be Sherwood green metallic, but that color had been replaced in 1963 by teal green. Rock Video International/BM*

▶ *Fender Telecaster, ocean turquoise metallic, 1965. This deep turquoise shade is one of the rarer custom colors. Hank Sable/BM*

◀ *Fender Esquire, charcoal frost metallic, 1967. Charcoal frost is lighter than black and has a metal flake content. Rod Norwood/WC*

▶ *Jazz bass, sonic blue, circa 1966. Sonic blue is the lightest of the blue colors of the 1960s. Chris Grocutt/BM*

► *Jazz Bass, sonic blue, 1965 (top right). The aging process shows that blue and yellow do indeed make green. Underneath the yellowed lacquer is a sonic blue finish. Pete Alenov/DL*

► *Jazzmaster, blue ice metallic, 1966 (bottom right). On this guitar the aged lacquer hides the subtle blue of the finish. In areas where the lacquer has worn away, the original shade of blue shows up as apparent highlights. Gruhn Guitars/WC*

▼ *Fender Telecaster, red mahogany, 1966. The rare red mahogany finish was never a custom color but was listed in the 1964–65 catalog as a standard option on the Telecaster, Esquire, Duo-Sonic, and Musicmaster. The penciled notation under the finish (above) refers, of course, to the finish color and not to the wood, which is ash. Toby Ruckert/WC*

◄ Fender Telecaster, floral blue, 1968. A catchphrase of the late 1960s, "flower power" comes to life on this companion to the pink paisley Telecaster. Pink paisley and floral blue finishes were also offered on the Telecaster Bass and were available in 1968 and 1969 only. Gil Southworth/BM

▼ Fender Telecaster, pink paisley, 1969. Out of the psychedelic era came the paisley finish, which is actually adhesive-backed paper oversprayed with a polyester clear coat. Exposure to air has aged the polyester, except under the pickguard where the original pink color holds true. Dave's Guitar Shop/BM

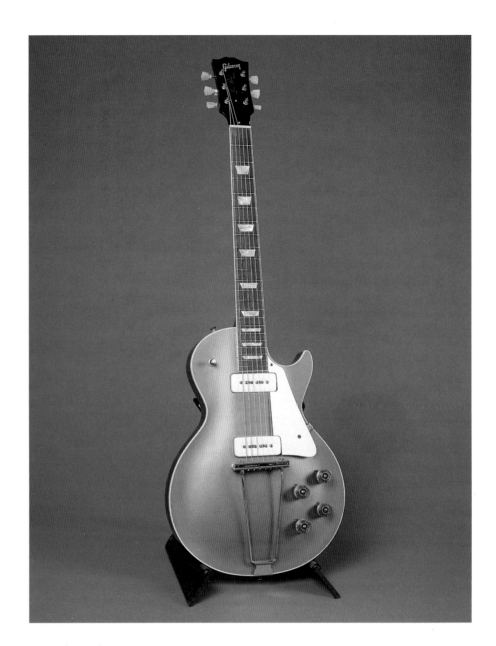

► *Gibson Les Paul Model, 1952. Gibson's first solid-body electric guitar was already in the final design stages when Les Paul was approached for an endorsement. One of Paul's two contributions, the gold top finish, is still a popular color on Les Pauls. His other, the combination bridge-tailpiece, did not fare so well. He designed it with the strings looping over the bridge, but the low rise of the Les Paul Model's top made it necessary to loop the strings under the bridge, which made it virtually impossible for players to mute the strings with the palm of the hand. The design was quickly replaced by a simpler one. Les Paul's endorsement eventually included 40 or more model variations—by far the most successful endorsement agreement in the history of fretted instruments. Gruhn Guitars/DL*

SOLIDBODIES
▼ ▼ ▼

Gibson

Gibson president Ted McCarty's initial reaction to Fender's solidbody guitar of 1950 was to laughingly refer to it as "the plank guitar." Within a year, however, McCarty and his staff were frantically trying to bring a Gibson solidbody to market.

As Gibson has throughout its history, the company made up for a late start with a flood of innovation and marketing. The new Gibson featured a carved top, contoured along the lines of an archtop guitar. To the player of a conventional archtop hollowbody, the arch of Gibson's new solidbody may have had a more familiar feel than that of the flat-bodied Fender, but the primary reason for the design was to give Gibson an aesthetic edge over the competition. An upstart company such as Fender would not be able to make carved-top guitars without a considerable investment in new tooling.

For an instant marketing push, Gibson sought the endorsement of Les Paul, who had been performing on his own homemade solidbody guitars for 10 years or more. The sense of urgency Gibson felt is shown by the very presence of an endorser—only the third in Gibson history. The earlier endorsement models, named after Nick Lucas and Roy Smeck, had last been made in the 1930s. Furthermore, Gibson put Les Paul's name on the new model despite the fact that Paul's design input was limited to the combination bridge-tailpiece and the gold top finish.

The Les Paul Model debuted in 1952 and by the end of 1955 was joined by three related models. Toward the end of the decade, however, sales began to slip, and in 1961 the body shapes were changed drastically. The new SG (for Solid Guitar) shape may have been designed to deal with two complaints about the original model: It had only a single cutaway (all Fenders after the Telecaster and Esquire were double-cutaway) and it was very heavy, with a mahogany body and maple top cap. The SG body was solid mahogany but thinner and lighter, and it had double cutaways with bold pointed horns. Although the SG models sold well, by the end of the 1960s enough customers were asking for Les Pauls that Gibson began reintroducing them.

Also in the early 1960s Gibson introduced a low-end solidbody line, the Melody Makers, and they sold quite well until the last years of the decade. The company had no such luck with new high-end models, however. In the late 1950s a series of radically shaped guitars made of korina wood (a trade name for African limba wood) was introduced, but the first two models—the Explorer and Flying V—sold so poorly that the line was discontinued before the third model could be produced. In the 1960s another new line appeared with an unusual body shape. The Firebirds were more popular than the korinas but not successful enough to survive the 1960s.

In the 1970s and 1980s Gibson introduced various new solidbody styles, but few are notable today. The 1950s-style carved-top Les Paul is once again the flagship of the Gibson solidbody line, with reissues of the korinas and Firebirds also selling well.

▲ *Gibson Les Paul Model, 1954. This "stud" version of the combination bridge-tail-piece, with strings wrapping over the bridge, appeared in 1953. It was not only simpler, but it was believed to provide a more solid anchor and thus more sustain than the earlier trapeze style. Strings West Tulsa/DL*

149

▶ *Gibson Les Paul Model, 1956. Most Les Pauls have a gold finish on the top only, with natural mahogany showing on the back and sides. A few have gold finish all over, including the back of the neck (below right). The tune-o-matic bridge with individually adjustable string saddles debuted with the Les Paul Custom in 1954 and was adopted on the Les Paul Model in mid 1955. Bob Christopher/DL*

▼ *Gibson Les Paul Standard, 1959. The Les Paul Model was quite successful for a few years, but, despite continual improvements in equipment, including double-coil humbucking pickups in mid 1957, sales fell steadily. In 1958 the gold gave way to cherry sunburst, and the model was renamed Les Paul Standard to distinguish it from the three other Les Pauls in the line. Sales picked up only slightly, and the entire line was severely overhauled in early 1961. John Clardy/BM*

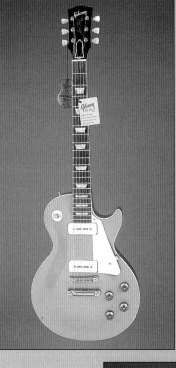

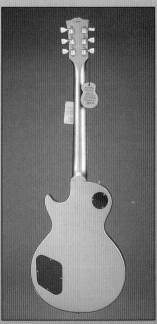

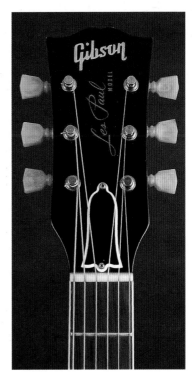

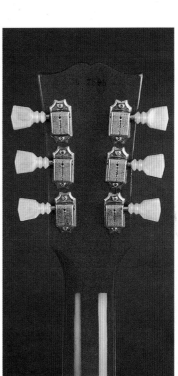

◀ *Gibson Les Paul Standard, 1960. The Les Paul Standard of 1958 to 1960 is one of the most highly sought guitars on the vintage market. The degree of "flame" or "tiger-stripe" wood grain in the top can mean thousands of dollars to collectors. Although this guitar is officially a Les Paul Standard, the peghead continues to bear the original name: Les Paul Model. Serial numbers from 1953 through 1960 are inked on the back of the peghead. During this period, the first digit of the number corresponds to the last digit of the year. Where the earlier goldtops show natural mahogany on the back and sides, the cherry stain on the Standard continues from the outer edges of the top all the way around the back of the body. Toby Ruckert/WC*

▶ Gibson Les Paul Junior, early 1958. In 1954 Gibson framed the Les Paul Model in the line with the Custom above it and the Les Paul Junior below. While the Junior's body outline is the same as the two higher models, it does not have a carved top. The pickup remains a P-90 after the higher models have gone to humbuckers, and the finish is a common sunburst. Gordon Dow/BM

▼ Gibson Les Paul Custom, 1956. The Les Paul Model grew into a line in 1954, topped by the Les Paul Custom. The Custom introduced the tune-o-matic bridge, which would eventually find its way across Gibson's entire high-end electric line. The bridge pickup is the same type as the white-covered "soapbar" P-90 of the gold-top. The neck pickup has nonadjustable rectangular pole pieces, and it has become known by its magnet type—Alnico V. The Custom is also known by several nicknames, including "Black Beauty" for its all-black finish and "Fretless Wonder" for its low frets. Gordon Dow/BM

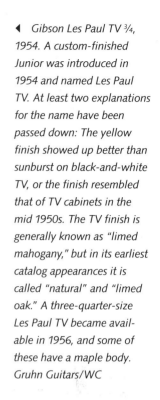

◀ Gibson Les Paul TV ¾, 1954. A custom-finished Junior was introduced in 1954 and named Les Paul TV. At least two explanations for the name have been passed down: The yellow finish showed up better than sunburst on black-and-white TV, or the finish resembled that of TV cabinets in the mid 1950s. The TV finish is generally known as "limed mahogany," but in its earliest catalog appearances it is called "natural" and "limed oak." A three-quarter-size Les Paul TV became available in 1956, and some of these have a maple body. Gruhn Guitars/WC

▶ Gibson Les Paul Custom, 1961. With the switch to humbucking pickups in mid 1957, the Les Paul Custom gained a third pickup. Hansen's Guitar Studio/M. Hansen

◀ Gibson Les Paul Junior,
1959. The Les Paul Junior
outsold the other three Les
Paul models combined.
Nevertheless, Gibson tried to
improve the Junior in mid-
1958 with a double-cutaway
body. The change in finish
from sunburst to cherry stain
probably represents a tie-in
with the cherry back and
sides of the Les Paul Standard of the same years.
The changes worked well for
the Junior. Shipping totals
almost doubled from 2,408
in 1958 to 4,364 in 1959,
making the Junior Gibson's
best-selling model—acoustic
or electric—and accounting
for one-eighth of the company's total instrument sales
that year. Rod Norwood/BM

▼ Gibson Les Paul Special,
1956. Yet another Les Paul
model appeared in 1955.
The Special is essentially a
TV model (limed mahogany
is the standard Special finish)
with two pickups and a
bound fingerboard. Bob
Christopher/DL

◀ Gibson "Les Paul/SG" Custom, 1962. Technically speaking, this model is a Les Paul Custom with SG body style because it retains a Les Paul reference (below). Like the Les Paul Custom it replaced, the SG Custom has three pickups. White was the standard finish for the Custom; this cherry stain was standard on the Standard but very rare on a Custom. The ebony tailblock appears on occasional examples. Bob Christopher/DL

▲ SG Special, late 1959. The success of the double-cutaway Les Paul Junior no doubt prompted Gibson to give the Les Paul Special the same shape in early 1959. For unknown reasons, the Special's model name was changed from Les Paul to SG in late 1959, but, except for the TV, none of the other Les Pauls became SGs until after the change to a more streamlined double-cutaway body in 1961. Bob Christopher/DL

◀ Gibson "Les Paul/SG"
Standard, 1961. In early 1961
a completely new body
shape appeared on all the
Les Paul models. The Standard, Custom, and Junior
did not receive the SG designation, however, until late
1963. Collectors refer to the
SG body examples from
1961 to 1963, which are still
marked "Les Paul," as "Les
Paul/SG" models. Jimmy
Wallace/BM

▼ Gibson "Les Paul/SG"
Custom tenor, 1963. The
customer who ordered this
instrument obviously wanted
Gibson's highest ornamentation, plus Bigsby vibrato,
on a solidbody tenor guitar.
Lloyd Chiate/BM

▲ *Gibson EB-0, 1960. After retiring the EB in 1958 Gibson introduced a cheaper bass in 1959, modeled after the double-cutaway version of the Les Paul Junior. By this time the EB-2 semi-hollowbody bass had been introduced. The new solidbody bass was not a higher-grade instrument than the EB-2 or the EB, so it was named EB-0. Gruhn Guitars/WC*

◀ *Gibson EB-3L, 1970. The double-pickup EB-3 was introduced in 1960 with the rounded-horn body of the Les Paul Junior. Like the solidbody guitars, solidbody basses changed to the pointed-horn SG-style body shape in the early 1960s. Gibson basses never gained the acceptance of the Fender Precision or Jazz models, and one reason may have been the scale length— 30½ inches compared with 34 inches on the high-end Fenders. In late 1969 Gibson introduced two long-scale models, the EB-3L and the EB-0L, but, even though they cost no more than the short-scale models, they were less successful. Gruhn Guitars/WC*

◀ *Gibson EB, 1953. As Fender followed the Telecaster guitar in 1950 with the Precision bass in 1951, so Gibson followed its 1952 solidbody guitar with a solidbody bass in 1953. The EB (for Electric Bass) sports a unique violin-shaped body and, like the Les Paul Model, a carved top. It was discontinued in 1958 and revived as the EB-1 from 1970 to 1972. Pittsburgh Guitars/BM*

▶ Gibson Les Paul Recording, 1977. To add to the confusion of Les Paul models in the late 1960s, a new family appeared with slightly larger bodies than earlier models and, like Les Paul's personal guitar, low-impedance pickups. Gruhn Guitars/WC

▶ Gibson Les Paul Deluxe, 1976. By the late 1960s Gibson recognized a growing demand for the old Les Paul but could not figure out exactly which version to revive. In 1968 a new Les Paul Standard with gold top finish and soapbar P-90 pickups (a version that had never officially been named Standard) and a new Les Paul Custom with two humbuckers were introduced. A year later the Standard was revamped with a four-piece "pancake" body and the mini-humbucking pickups used on Gibson's Epiphone line. It was then renamed the Les Paul Deluxe. In 1971 the Les Paul Standard '58 was introduced, but it was more similar to a 1954 model. Finally, in 1976 a Les Paul Standard appeared that came close to the original, and it was eventually expanded into a line with variations including less trim (Les Paul Studio), lighter weight and less trim (Les Paul Studio Lite), cherry sunburst finish (Classic), and a full-blown reissue of the 1956, 1957, 1959, and 1960 models. Gruhn Guitars/WC

▲ Gibson Les Paul Artisan. A fancy version of the Les Paul with banjo-style "hearts and flowers" fingerboard inlay debuted in 1976 and lasted through 1981. Gruhn Guitars/WC

▶ Gibson 25th Anniversary Les Paul, 1979. This special-order model featured a flamed maple top and Super 400–style fingerboard inlay. The peghead ornamentation commemorates the Les Paul Custom's 25th anniversary and Les Paul's 50th anniversary as a performer. Gruhn Guitars/WC

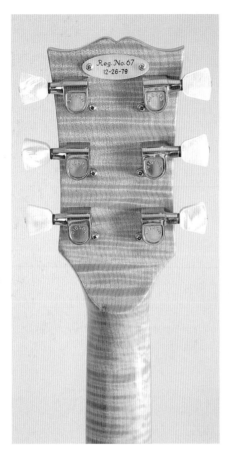

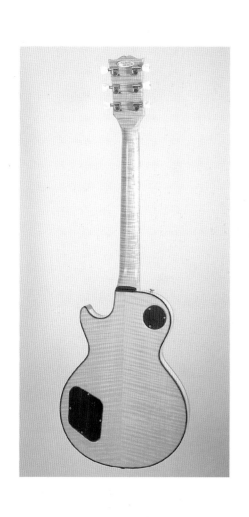

◀ Gibson The Les Paul, 1979. The ultimate in a fancy Les Paul, called The Les Paul, was offered from 1976 through 1979. The knobs, bindings, pickup frames, backplates, and even the selector switch cap are of rosewood. The metal parts, except for the tailpiece string anchors and knobs, are gold-plated. The fingerboard is ebony and rosewood, and the inlay is abalone. The finest tiger-stripe maple is used for the top, back, and neck. A mother-of-pearl plate on the back of the peghead is engraved with a registered serial number and the date. Gruhn Guitars/WC

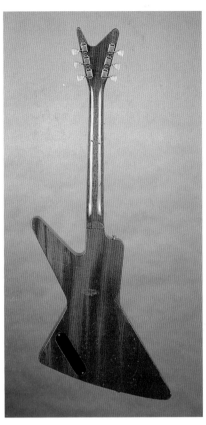

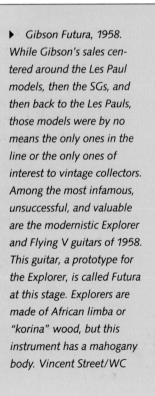

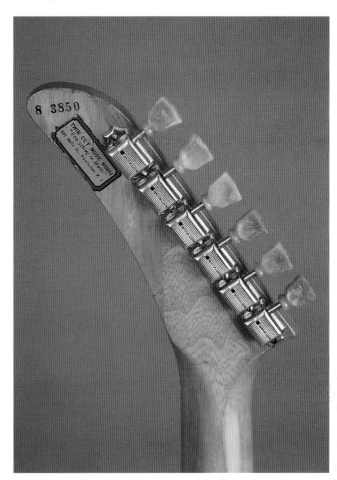

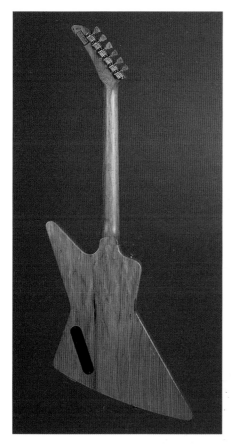

◀ *Gibson Explorer, 1958. In contrast to the smooth, rounded body lines of virtually every model from any manufacturer prior to 1958, the Explorer features sharp angles and extended body bouts. Gibson shipping totals do not specifically list the Explorer, but shipping records for the "Korina (Mod. Gtr.)" show nineteen instruments in 1958 and three in 1959, making this one of Gibson's rarest and most highly sought production models. The first digit 8 in the serial number (above) indicates a 1958 production date. Kunio Kishida/WC*

▲ Gibson Moderne, 1982.
Although some collectors
speculate wishfully that the
"Korina (Mod. Gtr.)" listed
on shipping records is the
Moderne, the model exists
only in an artist's rendering
and a patent drawing.
Not one 1958 Moderne has
ever surfaced. It was "reissued" in 1982 along with
reissues of the Explorer and
Flying V. The reissue korina
models were only slightly
more successful than the
originals, and they, too, have
attracted the interest of
collectors. Gary Dick/BM

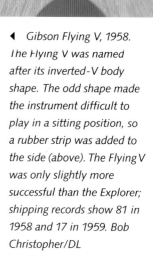

◀ Gibson Flying V, 1958.
The Flying V was named
after its inverted-V body
shape. The odd shape made
the instrument difficult to
play in a sitting position, so
a rubber strip was added to
the side (above). The Flying V
was only slightly more
successful than the Explorer;
shipping records show 81 in
1958 and 17 in 1959. Bob
Christopher/DL

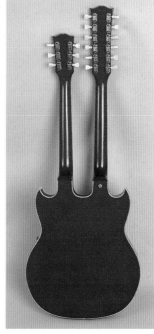

◀ Gibson EDS-1275, 1961. Gibson introduced two doubleneck models in 1958 with a unique body style: double pointed cutaways with carved top and, despite the lack of soundholes, a fully hollow body. The EDS-1275 has standard six- and twelve-string necks; the second model, cataloged as the EMS-1235 Double Mandolin, has a short-scale, six-string guitar neck along with a standard guitar neck. Both catalog models were available by custom order only, and in reality any combination of necks—including mandolin, tenor, or plectrum—was available. Wine red finish was at this time a rare custom-ordered feature. Crawford White/WC

▲ *Gibson Firebird I, 1964. Gibson's second attempt at a radical new solidbody shape came in mid-1963 with the Firebird line. Four models, plus two Thunderbird basses, made up the family. In trim and electronics the four Firebirds followed the Junior-Special-Standard-Custom scheme of the Les Paul and SG lines. Among the new features are the "reverse" body and peghead styles, banjo-type tuners, neck-through-body construction, and mini-humbucking pickups with no visible pole pieces. Bob Christopher/DL*

▼ *Gibson EBS-1250, 1961. The EBSF-1250 with bass neck and guitar neck did not appear on shipping totals or in catalogs until 1962. At that time doubleneck models switched to a fully solid SG-style body. Furthermore, the catalog model has a fuzztone feature (denoted by the F in the model name), which this example lacks. The rounded horns were "introduced" after a factory employee became sick on the job and left the body template on the Schriber press, where the pointed horns burned off. Fly By Night/BM*

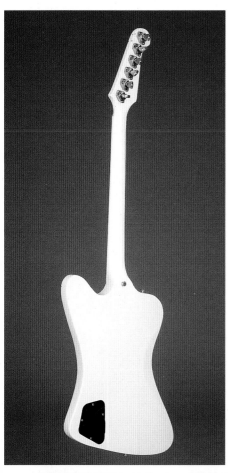

◀ Gibson Firebird III, 1963. Gibson called this finish Polaris white. The earliest Firebirds have six tuners on the treble side of the peghead (below left), and they are straight-through, banjo style (below center). Bob Christopher/DL

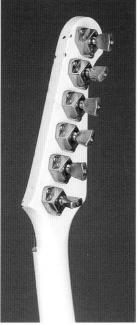

▼ Gibson Firebird III, 1964. Possibly because of its two pickups and vibrato, the Firebird III was more successful than the cheaper Firebird I. This bronze metallic finish is not among the standard Gibson custom colors. Bob Christopher/DL

▶ *Gibson custom color chart, 1963. With the Firebirds Gibson followed Fender's lead and offered an array of custom finish colors. Unlike Fender, however, Gibson offered these colors only on Firebirds, and the offering was more limited— 10 Gibson colors compared with 14 for Fender. Bob Christopher/DL*

▼ *Gibson Firebird VII, 1964. The top of the Firebird line, the VII, has three pickups and gold-plated metal parts. This example has a frost blue finish. Wagner Swanson/BM*

▲ Gibson Firebird V, 1965. As the trapezoidal fingerboard inlay suggests, the Firebird V corresponds roughly to the Les Paul Standard and SG Standard. This finish is Kerry green. Gruhn Guitars/DL

▶ Gibson Thunderbird IV, 1965. Firebird models are odd-numbered; the companion Thunderbird basses take up the even numbers. The Thunderbird II has one pickup; the Thunderbird IV has two. This example is cardinal red. Jacksonville Guitars/SE

▲ Gibson Firebird VII, 1965. After May 1965 the Firebird was revamped with an opposite and less angular shape, known to collectors as the "non-reverse" body. The original peghead configuration with tuners on the treble side had proven awkward and had already been reversed before the body shape was changed. A glued-in neck replaced the neck-through-body construction of the earlier version. The changes did not perk up the dwindling sales of all Firebirds, and the last ones were shipped in 1969. This example sports the Pelham blue finish. Gruhn Guitars/DL

▲ Gibson Chet Atkins CE, 1993. Chet Atkins switched allegiance from Gretsch to Gibson in 1981. His first Gibson model, the Chet Atkins CE (for Classical Electric), is a solidbody guitar with nylon strings, a classical neck, and a "piezo" pickup under the bridge. The sound-hole is strictly cosmetic. A steel-string version, the SST, debuted in 1987. Gruhn Guitars/WC

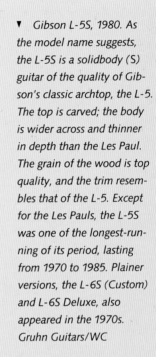

▼ Gibson L-5S, 1980. As the model name suggests, the L-5S is a solidbody (S) guitar of the quality of Gibson's classic archtop, the L-5. The top is carved; the body is wider across and thinner in depth than the Les Paul. The grain of the wood is top quality, and the trim resembles that of the L-5. Except for the Les Pauls, the L-5S was one of the longest-running of its period, lasting from 1970 to 1985. Plainer versions, the L-6S (Custom) and L-6S Deluxe, also appeared in the 1970s. Gruhn Guitars/WC

SOLIDBODIES
▼ ▼ ▼

Gretsch

Although Gretsch is best known for 1950s hollowbody electrics, the company did not lag far behind Fender and Gibson in putting solidbody models into production. The Gretsch Duo-Jet that appeared in mid 1953 bore numerous similarities to Gibson's Les Paul, including a single-cutaway body shape, contoured (carved) top, mahogany body with maple top cap, finish color on the top and natural mahogany showing on the back and sides, and two pickups.

The Gretsch solidbody had one significant difference hidden under the top, however. Whereas the Les Paul was routed only enough to accommodate the electronics, the Duo-Jet was heavily routed under the top cap, probably to reduce weight. But the extra routing, along with the DeArmond pickups, gave the Duo-Jet a distinct sound different from either a Fender or a Gibson.

Unlike Fender and Gibson, which had two well-defined solidbody guitar designs by 1954, Gretsch's solidbody "line" throughout the 1950s was essentially one guitar with cosmetic differences delineating models. In 1961, the same year the body shape changed from single- to double-cutaway, a new model with a new body shape appeared. A third body shape emerged in 1965, and no others were introduced through the 1960s. By contrast, Fender and Gibson had twice as many distinct solidbody styles in the late 1960s.

Under new ownership in the 1970s, Gretsch finally responded to the popularity of solidbody electrics and expanded the offering, but no solidbodies of the 1970s or even the 1960s rival the original Duo-Jet style in popularity among players or collectors today.

▶ *Gretsch Duo-Jets, right-handed (left), 1956, and left-handed, 1958. Like other Gretsch models, the Duo-Jet series changed constantly, as shown by the Melita bridge and block inlays on the 1956 example and the roller bridge and thumbprint inlay on the 1958 version. The left-hand-ed fingerboard was originally inlaid for a right-handed guitar, thus the double thumbprints. Like Gibson's Les Pauls, the mahogany back and sides have a clear finish. Scott Jennings/BM*

◀ Gretsch Duo-Jet tenor guitar, 1955. Television star Arthur Godfrey popularized the baritone ukulele in the late 1950s. Gretsch took advantage of the interest in four-string guitars by adding a solidbody tenor guitar and a baritone ukulele to the Duo-Jet line in 1954. The uke disappeared immediately; the tenor last appeared on a 1959 price list. Gruhn Guitars/WC

▼ Gretsch Jet Firebird, 1959. The Jet Firebird is a Duo-Jet in red with black back and sides that debuted in 1955. Jay Levin/BM

▼ *Gretsch Round-Up, 1956, and Electromatic Twin amplifier, mid 1950s. The Round-Up, introduced in 1954, has standard Duo-Jet electronics but is trimmed in deluxe Western style. A large piece of metal modeled after a Western belt buckle covers the string anchors. Tooled leather is used for side trim, strap, amplifier trim, and case trim. A G has been branded into the top, and Western motifs adorn the peghead, pickguard, and fingerboard inlay. Because of its similarities to the Chet Atkins Solid Body, the Round-Up was dropped in 1961 with the advent of double-cutaway Duo-Jets. Kenton Schneider/BM*

◀ *Gretsch Chet Atkins Solid Body, 1954 (facing page, top right). The solid companion to the Chet Atkins Hollow Body debuted in 1954. The only differences between it and the Round-Up are standard Chet Atkins model features: Bigsby vibrato, nonadjustable bridge; signature pickguard; and (except for this example) metal nut. Early examples of both models have a knotty pine top (above) and no inlay at the first fret (left). Chet Atkins/DL*

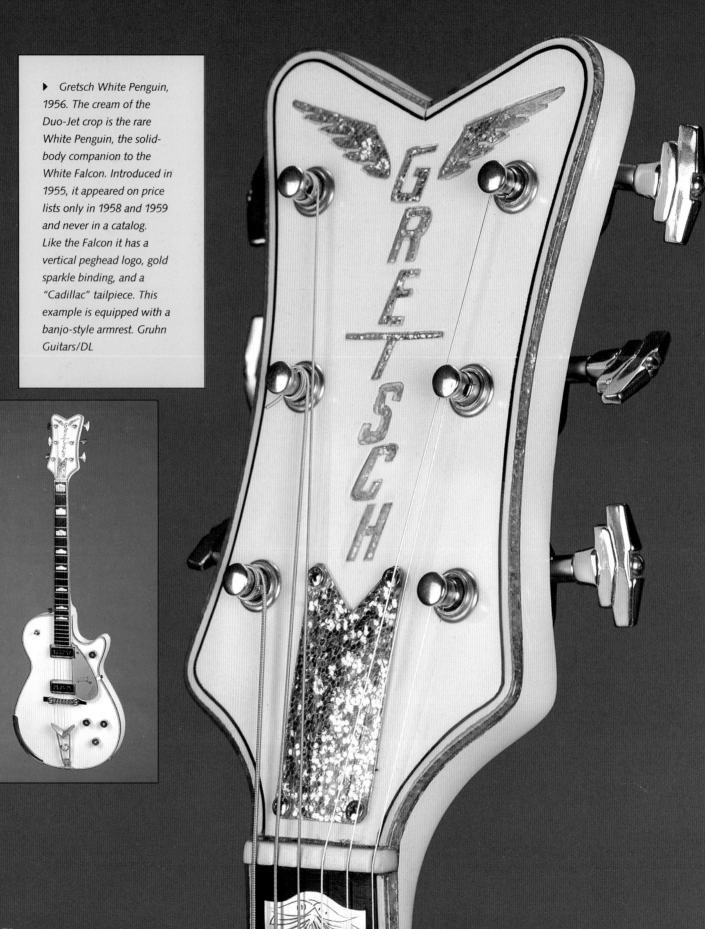

▶ Gretsch White Penguin, 1956. The cream of the Duo-Jet crop is the rare White Penguin, the solid-body companion to the White Falcon. Introduced in 1955, it appeared on price lists only in 1958 and 1959 and never in a catalog. Like the Falcon it has a vertical peghead logo, gold sparkle binding, and a "Cadillac" tailpiece. This example is equipped with a banjo-style armrest. Gruhn Guitars/DL

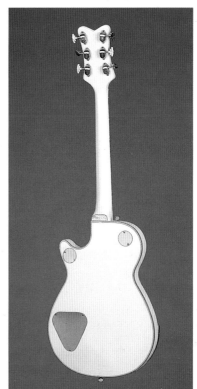

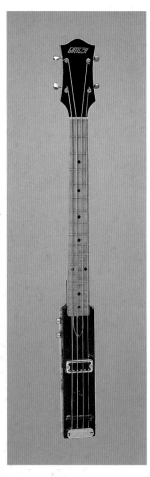

▶ Gretsch Bikini, 1961.
A doubleneck guitar that can
break down into two sepa-
rate instruments! It sounds
like a great idea but it never
found a market, and the Bikini was offered only in 1961
and 1962. The guitar and the
bass slide into place. When
they are removed, the back
folds up. The guitar and bass
were also available individually. Gruhn Guitars/DL

▼ Gretsch Corvette "Gold Duke," circa 1966. The Corvette variations included an upscale model in the mid 1960s. The Duke sported metallic flecks in the paint finish and was available in either gold or silver. Peter Ilowite/WC

▲ Gretsch Corvette, 1963, owned by Robert Nighthawk. The Corvette appeared in 1963 and was Gretsch's first low-end solidbody. It was available with one or two pickups, with or without vibrato. Memphis Music and Blues Museum/WC

▼ Gretsch Champagne Sparkle Jet, 1963. The Duo-Jet series went to a double-cutaway shape in 1961, probably in reaction to Gibson's double-cutaway SG series. Guitars at Large/BM

179

▶ *Gretsch Hi-Roller, 1976. In 1976 Gretsch developed a new solidbody for Chet Atkins with its own distinct body shape and Gibson-style humbucking pickups. No more than eight prototypes, and possibly as few as three or four, were made. The dice on the fingerboard add up to the fret position where they are placed. Presumably because of the gambling association, the production models debuted as the Atkins Axe and the Super Axe, both minus the dice. Dean Turner/BM*

◀ *Rickenbacker Combo 800, 1956. The early Combo 800 is visually distinguishable from the Combo 600 only by its two selector switches. The 800 pickup, however, has two coils and is a humbucker when both coils are selected. Although the Combo 800 was introduced three years before Gibson's first humbucking pickup, Rickenbacker failed to capitalize on this technological advance. In fact, Rick replaced the humbucker with two separate single-coil pickups on the Combo 800 in late 1957. The backplate covers routings in the body for weight reduction. Lloyd Chiate/BM*

SOLIDBODIES

▼   ▼   ▼

Rickenbacker

In 1953 Adolph Rickenbacker sold his company to F. C. Hall, founder of the Radio-Tel electronics distributing company (and at the time a partner in Fender's distribution company, Fender Sales). The sale marked the end not only of a pioneering career but also of the Hawaiian guitar era at Rickenbacker. From 1932 through the early 1950s Hawaiians dominated the line; Ricken-

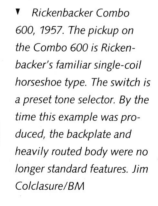

backer never had more than one electric hollowbody model available at any given time, and the bodies for those models were bought from other makers. F. C. Hall immediately shifted emphasis to modern solidbody standard guitars, starting with the Combo 600 and Combo 800 in 1954 and adding the 4000 bass in 1957.

The body shapes of these and later Rick models—hollowbody as well as solid—were unique when they appeared. And they are still unique. Even the more familiar and successful models have never been copied by other manufacturers in the way that the Telecaster, Stratocaster, and Les Paul models have been.

The Combo solidbodies were eclipsed after 1958 by Rickenbacker's Capri line of thin hollowbody models that continue to be the mainstays of the Rickenbacker guitar line today. In the bass market, however, the opposite was true. Rickenbacker's solidbody basses maintain a loyal following while the hollow models have never been as highly respected among players or collectors.

▼ *Rickenbacker Combo 600, 1957. The pickup on the Combo 600 is Rickenbacker's familiar single-coil horseshoe type. The switch is a preset tone selector. By the time this example was produced, the backplate and heavily routed body were no longer standard features. Jim Colclasure/BM*

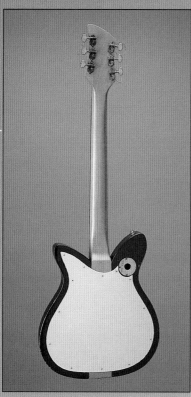

▲ *Rickenbacker Combo
450, 1957 (far right). In 1956
Rickenbacker introduced
a second body style—a
double-cutaway with a tulip
shape—on the single-pickup
Combo 400 and the double-
pickup Combo 450. The treble-side cutaway was deep-
ened in 1957. The backplate
(above) does not hide the
neck-through-body construction—a feature that would
later enhance Rickenbacker
solidbody basses. Wagner
Swanson/BM*

▶ *Rickenbacker Combo
800, 1957. In 1957 turquoise
joined blond as a standard
finish on the Combo models.
Shane's Music/BM*

▲ *Rickenbacker 4001, 1985 (above and far left). Ricken-backer introduced deluxe trim—body binding and tri-angular fingerboard inlay—on a hollowbody line in 1958, but these touches did not reach the solidbodies until 1961. The 4001 bass, introduced in late 1961, is a double-pickup, deluxe-trim version of the 4000. Gruhn Guitars/WC*

◄ *Rickenbacker Combo 450, mid-1960s. The red sunburst finish known as Fireglo was a standard option on the Combo 450 by 1960 and went on to become one of Rickenbacker's most popular finishes. The cresting wave body became the dom-inant style in the solidbody line; variations included single pickup (425), deluxe trim (460), or 12-string (450-12). Montana AI/BM*

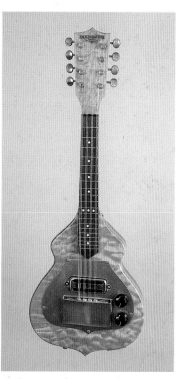

◄ Rickenbacker Combo 450, late 1950s. In 1958 the Combo 450 body changed yet again. The "cresting wave" shape lasted as long as the model did, until 1984. Guitar Tracker/BM

▶ Rickenbacker 4000, late 1950s. Rickenbacker's first bass, the 4000, was introduced in 1957. The cresting wave motif that would appear shortly on the body of the Combo 450 guitar graces the peghead of all solidbody basses. Although the horseshoe pickup gave way to a more conventional understring style in 1964, the body shape and neck-through-body construction remain the foundation of the Rickenbacker bass line. Lloyd Chiate/BM

◄ Rickenbacker Electric Mandolin, late 1950s. Rickenbacker offered a solidbody mandolin in 1958, available with four, five, or eight strings. The maple top and walnut back make it an attractive instrument despite its squat shape, but only nine of these were sold. Crawford White/WC

▶ *National Glenwood, 1955.*
National, a pioneer in prewar
electrics, made an early entry
into the postwar solidbody
market. The first Nationals,
introduced in 1953, had
a rather simple slab-body
design. The Glenwood, intro-
duced in 1954, went after
the high-end market with a
bank of control knobs, fancy
"butterfly" fingerboard inlay,
and natural finish. J. Gravity
Strings/BM

SOLIDBODIES
▼ ▼ ▼

Other Makers

As with lap steels, the sound production of a solidbody Spanish-style electric guitar is not affected by body shape so long as the bridge-neck-peghead connection is rigid. And like lap steel designers of an earlier era, solidbody designers were free to follow their imaginations.

▶ *National Glenwood 95,
1962. In 1962 National
brought out a new material,
Res-o-glas (fiberglass), and a
new body shape that roughly
resembles a map of the
United States. The Res-o-glas
guitars are not fully solid;
the bodies are made of two
pieces of molded fiberglass
joined by plastic edge binding. Three map-shaped
model groups were intro-
duced, each including three
models. The Glenwoods,
with butterfly fingerboard
inlay, were the fanciest.
Rick King/BM*

◀ *National Newport 84,
1963. The Newport series,
originally called Val-Pro,
sports quarter-circle fingerboard inlay. The finish was
sprayed into the mold before
the fiberglass was poured in
so that the body halves came
out with the finish already
applied. The Newport 84
is seafoam green. Model 82,
the lowest model of the
Newport group, has a "scar-
let" finish as a Val-Pro, "pep-
per red" under the Newport
name. Jay Levin/BM*

▶ *National Newport 88, 1964. Some map-shapes came with a special form-fitting case. The raven black Newport 88 is the highest of the three Newport models. Clifford Antone/BM*

◀ *National Westwood 75, 1963. The Westwood 75 is the only map-shaped National with a sunburst finish. The presence of a pickup built into the bridge puts it a step above the single-pickup Westwood 72. Strings West Tulsa/BM*

▶ *National Westwood 77, 1964. The wire coming from the bridge indicates the presence of a pickup—one of the last in a long list of innovative ideas from National. Like most of the company's post–World War II innovations, this one did not work very well. Although the map-shapes are considered by collectors to be the ultimate in cheap/cool guitars, they were not all that cheap when new, and National stopped making them in 1965. Cohn Rude/BM*

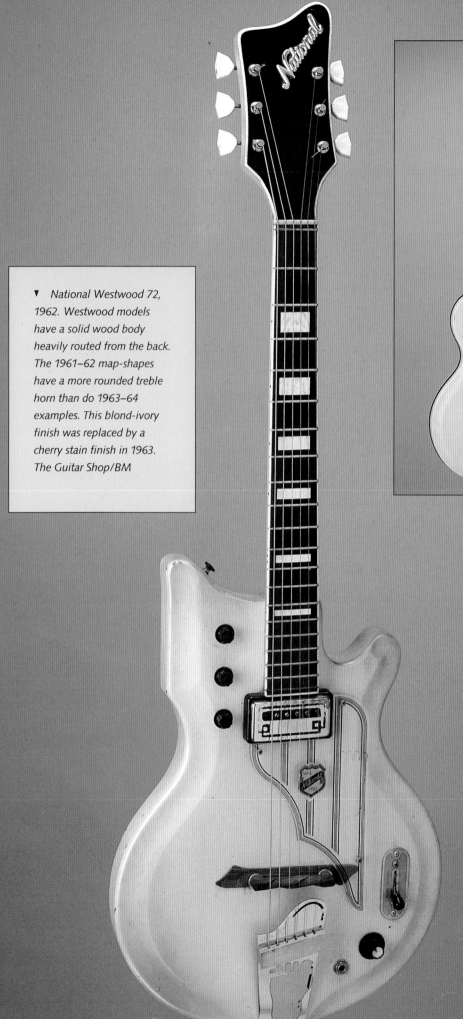

▼ *National Westwood 72, 1962. Westwood models have a solid wood body heavily routed from the back. The 1961–62 map-shapes have a more rounded treble horn than do 1963–64 examples. This blond-ivory finish was replaced by a cherry stain finish in 1963. The Guitar Shop/BM*

▲ *National Studio 66, 1962. National called this color "desert sand" or "desert buff." Collectors call it "flesh." The model was available in this version only from 1961 to 1963. Real Guitars/BM*

► *Danelectro U-2, 1956. Nathan (Nat) Daniel made amplifiers for Epiphone in New York in the 1940s and started his own company, Danelectro, in 1946 in Red Bank, New Jersey. In 1954 he developed a guitar for Sears to sell under its Silvertone brand and a year later marketed the first Danelectro brand guitars. His earliest instruments were made of solid wood, but by the time this example appeared he had come up with a cheap but functional semi-solid construction, with a top and back of ⅜-inch Masonite and only the perimeter shell, neck block, and bridge block of pine wood. The pickup coils are enclosed in lipstick tubes acquired from a cosmetics supply house. This guitar design, which was also available in such colors as fuchsia and peach, remained the quintessential Danelectro until 1969, when Nat Daniel made the last Danelectros. Kevin Murphy/BM*

▲ *Danelectro Longhorn six-string bass, late 1950s. Nat Daniel is one of the least-acknowledged innovators in the electric guitar business. He made the first tremolo amplifier in 1947 and the first reverb unit for guitar in 1950. In 1956 he scored another first with a six-string bass guitar. Two years later he came up with the extended-cutaway "longhorn" body style for four- and six-string basses, plus a guitar version called the Guitarlin. The six-string Longhorn bass has a 25-fret neck; the Guitarlin has a 30-fret neck. Pittsburgh Guitars/BM*

◄ Danelectro doubleneck guitar and bass, early 1960s. Despite the light body construction, the Danelectro design could withstand the extra string tension of a doubleneck instrument. The "stacked" pot design, another efficiency concept from Nat Daniel, puts volume and tone controls on the same shaft. Pittsburgh Guitars/BM

▼ Danelectro bass, late 1960s. The old "Coke bottle" peghead shape has given way to this stretched-out Fender-style peghead, but the basic design, including the lipstick-tube pickup, has changed little since the 1956 models. Gruhn Guitars/DL

▼ Coral and Danelectro sitars, late 1960s. When Beatles guitarist George Harrison took an interest in Indian music, the sitar became a rock and roll instrument. In typical efficient fashion Nat Daniel made an electric guitar sound like a sitar by extending the bridge surface so that the strings buzzed. In late 1967 Danelectro introduced the Coral brand so that the company would have a line to compete with its highly successful Sears Silvertone products. The Coral sitar, endorsed by guitarist Vincent Bell, features a rack of 13 sympathetically vibrating drone strings. The plainer six-string version was marketed under the Danelectro brand. Gruhn Guitars/DL

◀ Silvertone, mid-1960s. Made by Danelectro and sold by Sears, Roebuck, this guitar with an amplifier built into the case was one of the more succcessful beginner's models of the 1960s. The outfit retailed for about $70. A two-pickup model with a more powerful, tremolo-equipped amplifier was also available. Vincent Street/WC

▲ Epiphone Coronet, 1959. Although the Epiphone brand name stood for high quality archtop guitars from the early 1930s to the mid 1950s, solidbodies and thinline archtops dominated the electric line after Gibson's parent company C.M.I. acquired Epi in 1957. The Fender Telecaster body inspired this early Gibson-made example; the cutaway is Tele-shaped with a mirror-image cutaway added on the bass side. Also like the Telecaster, the earliest Coronets have this "slab" body. Body edges became rounded beginning in 1959. Conchord/BM

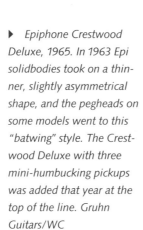

▶ Epiphone Crestwood Deluxe, 1965. In 1963 Epi solidbodies took on a thinner, slightly asymmetrical shape, and the pegheads on some models went to this "batwing" style. The Crestwood Deluxe with three mini-humbucking pickups was added that year at the top of the line. Gruhn Guitars/WC

▶ *Guild Polara S-100, 1963. Collectors now refer to the Polara's body shape as the "melted Hershey bar" style, and perhaps it was difficult to fit this asymmetrical body on a guitar stand. For whatever reason, Guild designers thought a built-in "kickstand" would help. Midtown/BM*

◀ Mosrite Ventures, circa 1963. Semie Moseley came up with this body shape by flipping a Fender Stratocaster over and tracing it. He built the first one for Nokie Edwards, lead guitarist of the Ventures, a popular instrumental group. Early Ventures guitars have a triple-bound top. Only the very earliest—this guitar has serial number 0050—actually have the lever-action "Vibra-mute" and the bridge saddle with the homemade look. The neck is glued-in; later examples have a bolted-on neck. Crawford White/WC

▼ Mosrite Ventures, circa 1963. By the time this example (serial number 0467) was made, the top had lost its binding, and, although the tailpiece (bottom) says "Vibra-mute" beneath the vibrato arm, the mute is gone for good from the Ventures model. J. P. Masahiro/BM

▼ *Mosrite Joe Maphis doubleneck, mid 1960s. California country guitarist Joe Maphis had Semie Moseley build him a double-neck guitar with a six-string and a twelve-string neck. It became a standard Mosrite model, one of several endorsed by Maphis. Dave Crocker/BM*

▲ *Mosrite doubleneck, circa 1963. Larry Collins, who with his sister Lorrie found rockabilly fame as the Collins Kids, played a Moseley-made doubleneck with a standard neck and a short-scale six-string neck. In production, however, it was one of the Joe Maphis models. Like the early Ventures examples, this guitar has the string mute and the bridge with the melted-down look. The knobs are not original. Cohn Rude/BM*

◀ Mosrite custom, 1980. Semie Moseley made this guitar just before his company moved from Bakersfield, California, to Carson City, Nevada, where it stayed only a year before moving on to North Carolina. "He just said that was the guitar he always wanted to make," recalls Robert Gentry, Moseley's business partner at the time. All the hardware was cast with the "lost wax investment" process. Moseley carved the original wood models and Gentry completed the process with rubber molds, wax models, casting-plaster molds, and final casting in bronze. The frets have a unique design intended to cut down neck vibration. They are all part of a single piece of metal, with a longitudinal connecting bar embedded in the neck. Robert Gentry/WC

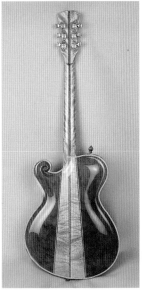

▲ Ampeg f-hole guitar, late 1960s. Ampeg was much more successful with amplifiers than with instruments. A solidbody bass with scrolled peghead (far right) and f-hole cutouts was one of the company's more memorable, if not successful, products. This guitar version was never put into production. Gruhn Guitars/WC

▶ Vega six-string tenor, mid 1960s. Although Vega had been a contender in the acoustic and electric archtop guitar markets prior to World War II, by the 1960s the company's reputation rested almost entirely on banjos. This solidbody tenor guitar, with the two high strings doubled, is one of the more unusual creations from any maker of the postwar years. Gruhn Guitars/WC

▲ Ampeg Dan Armstrong guitar, 1969, and fretless bass, circa 1970, with Ludwig drum set, 1978. National and other makers had been using clear plastic, known by its trade name Lucite, for Hawaiian guitar fingerboards since the late 1940s. It seems inevitable that a company would eventually build an entire guitar body out of the material. Dan Armstrong designed the guitar and bass with a variety of interchangeable pickups, and Ampeg marketed them. A set of Lucite drums completes the see-through band set. Jacksonville Guitars/SE

▼ Gittler, early 1980s. "Skeleton body" would be a more accurate description than "solidbody" for these minimalist guitars, hand-built by Alan Gittler from 1978 to 1985. After Gittler moved to Israel in 1985, the Bar-Rashi company began marketing a production version with a more substantial body. Gruhn Guitars/WC

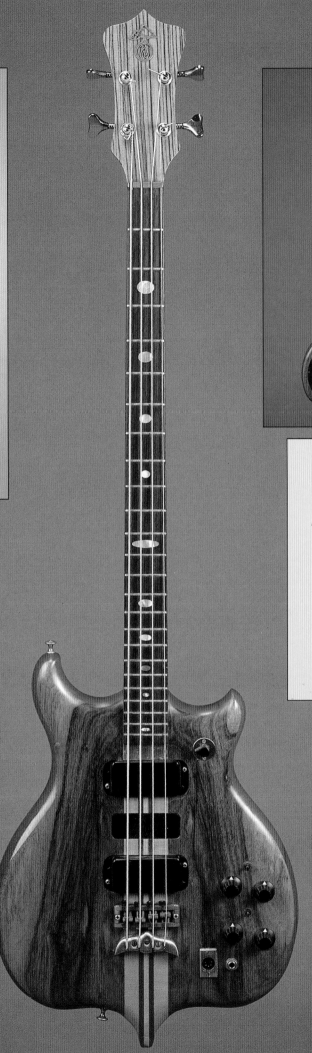

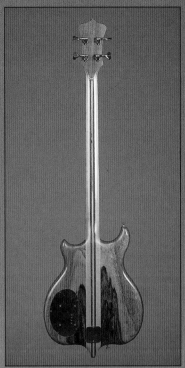

▲ Micro-Frets Husky bass, 1972. Micro-Frets made guitars and basses in Frederick, Maryland, beginning in 1965, and the company's most popular models were thinline semi-hollowbodies. The Husky bass appeared just before the company's demise in 1972. Gruhn Guitars/WC

▼ Alembic bass, 1977. This bass fills many of the demands of a professional player. The matched grain of the wood gives it an elegant traditional look. Neck-through-body construction provides maximum solidity. An additional jack allows direct output for studio recording. Mark O'Connor/DL

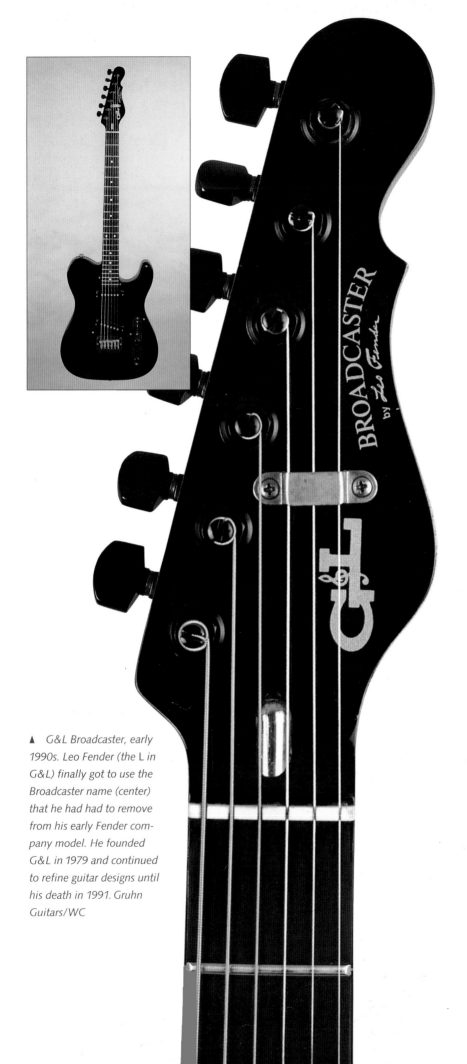

▼ Holmes Bo Diddley
Cadillac, late 1980s. Blues
singer Bo Diddley had several bizarre guitars made for
him by the Gretsch company,
and the Cadillac model,
named because of its resemblance to a tail fin, was
recreated by Nashville luthier
Tom Holmes. Among the
controls is a microchip that
plays digital recordings of
Diddley's famous sayings.
Bob Christopher/WC

▲ G&L Broadcaster, early
1990s. Leo Fender (the L in
G&L) finally got to use the
Broadcaster name (center)
that he had had to remove
from his early Fender company model. He founded
G&L in 1979 and continued
to refine guitar designs until
his death in 1991. Gruhn
Guitars/WC

▲ Steinberger bass, late 1980s. Like many inventors, Ned Steinberger was not the first to make what he popularized. Others had made headless instruments with tuners at the bridge (Les Paul built a headless guitar in the 1940s; Magnatone marketed a headless lap steel in the 1950s), but Steinberger's basses, introduced in 1982, have been by far the most successful. Additional innovations include a body and neck made of "graphite" (epoxy resin strengthened with carbon and glass fibers) and built-in pre-amps. Gruhn Guitars/WC

▼ B. C. Rich Mockingbird, 1986. Bernardo Chavez Rico started as a maker of classical and flamenco guitars in Los Angeles. After repairing Bo Diddley's rectangular Gretsch guitar, he became interested in electrics. Working with designer Neil Moser, Rico came up with several unique models, including the Mockingbird. Gruhn Guitars/WC

THINBODIES

▼   ▼   ▼

Gibson

In 1955 Gibson took the first step toward a new style of electric guitar that would incorporate features of the radical new solidbody models without offending tradition-conscious archtop players. From a head-on view, the new guitar looked like a normal, single-cutaway, *f*-hole archtop electric. But the body was about an inch thinner—2¼ inches compared with 3⅜—than a traditional archtop electric and thus easier to hold. The thinbody offered little acoustical capability, but Gibson's full-depth models, like the L-5CES or Super 400CES, had already lost most of their acoustic sound when pickups were mounted into the top, so the thinbody's lack of acoustics was not considered a drawback.

Once the thinner body gained acceptance among archtop players, Gibson took several more steps, further thinning the body to a depth of only 1 ⅝ inches and adding a cutaway on the bass side. A less visible but much more significant change took place under the top. The top of an electric archtop, even with pickups stifling most of the vibrations, still caused more feedback with less sustaining power than a solidbody guitar, so Gibson placed a block of wood under the top to stabilize it. The new semi-hollow guitar was dubbed the ES-335 and introduced in 1958. With its family of double-cutaway models, it became the standard-bearer of the semi-hollow style.

▶ *ES-225TDN, circa 1956. Gibson's first thinbody model, introduced in 1955, has the body shape and electronics of the popular full-depth ES-175, but its dot fingerboard inlay and the single layer of binding around the top make it plainer than the full-depth model, and it lacks the ES-175's crown peghead inlay. The only other difference is the tailpiece. This combination bridge-tailpiece debuted on the Les Paul model in 1952 but by 1955 was in use only on the ornate ES-295—never on the ES-175. The fact that this model was not considered by Gibson to be the thinline equivalent of the ES-175 became obvious in 1957, when the ES-175 was fitted with humbucking pickups while the ES-225T stayed with the P-90. The ES-225T was last made in 1959. Clifford Antone/BM*

▲ Gibson Byrdland, 1962. Like other high-end models, the Byrdland received humbucking pickups in 1957, and the cutaway was changed to a Florentine pointed shape in 1960. This example has the model's standard triple-loop tailpiece. The Byrdland was last made in 1993. Jim Colclasure/DL

▼ Gibson ES-350T, 1958. The middle model of the 1958 thinlines, the ES-350T also has the short scale of the Byrdland. It was only moderately successful but gained some notoriety as the model played by pioneer rock and roller Chuck Berry in the 1950s. It was discontinued in 1963, reintroduced in 1977 with a 1¾-inch body depth and a 25½-inch scale, and discontinued again in 1981. Clifford Antone/BM

▲ *Gibson ES-140T, 1957. This thin version of Gibson's three-quarter-size electric archtop appeared in 1956. It drove the full-depth version out of production in two years and lasted in the line until 1968. Gruhn Guitars/WC*

▼ *Gibson L-5CT with pickups, 1961. This thinbodied L-5C (for cutaway) is commonly known as the George Gobel model, after the comedian who custom-ordered the first of this style in 1959. Although offered as an acoustic guitar, most L-5CTs have either top-mounted pickups or a McCarty finger-rest pickup. A total of 43 were made between 1959 and 1961. Tim Kummer/BM*

▶ *Gibson ES-125TC (right).*
The low-end ES-125, a non-
cutaway model, was by far
the biggest seller of Gibson's
full-depth electric archtop
line in the early 1950s. When
a thinbody version, the
ES-125T, was introduced in
1956, it immediately domi-
nated sales of thinbody mod-
els. A double-pickup model
and a three-quarter-size
model appeared the next
year. A cutaway thinbody
with one or two pickups was
added in 1960, and it rivaled
the noncutaway version in
popularity. All versions of
the ES-125 were discontin-
ued in 1971. Gruhn Gui-
tars/WC

▼ *Gibson ES-335TD, 1958.*
The ES-335, introduced in
1958, sported a new body
shape with double rounded
cutaways and semi-hollow-
body construction. It was
an immediate success and is
still a mainstay of Gibson's
electric line. Jackque
Mazzoleni/BM

207

▶ *Gibson ES-335TD, 1964. The small block fingerboard inlay appeared on ES-335s in mid 1964. The shorter pickguard debuted in 1960, and a coil-tap switch was added in 1977. By 1982 Gibson realized that players as well as collectors preferred the earliest version of the ES-335, and the existing model was replaced by the ES-335DOT, with dot inlay, stop tailpiece, and no coil tap. Strings West Tulsa/BM*

▼ *Gibson ES-335TDC, 1959. Cherry finish ("C" stands for cherry rather than cutaway in this case) was an option in 1959, and it became the most common finish on ES-335–style guitars. Examples made prior to mid 1962, when the "PAF" (patent applied for) stickers on the back of the pickups were replaced by patent number stickers and the dot inlay gave way to small blocks, are the models most highly sought by collectors. Examples with the stop tailpiece are also more highly regarded than those of mid 1964 and after, which have a trapeze tailpiece as standard equipment. Clifford Antone/BM*

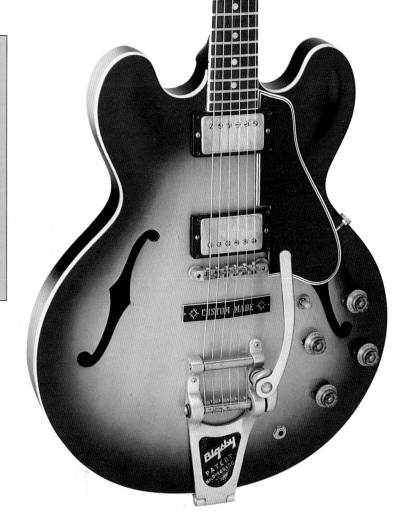

◀ Gibson ES-335TD-12, 1965. The folk music boom of the early 1960s brought 12-string acoustic guitars into vogue. When folkies picked up electrics, Gibson introduced electric 12-strings. With total sales of 2,062 from 1965 to 1970, the ES-335TD-12 was by far the most successful of Gibson's electric 12-string models (all the others were solidbodies). Gruhn Guitars/DL

▶ Gibson ES-335TD, 1960. The Bigsby vibrato tailpiece was optional on the ES-335, and on guitars fitted with a Bigsby Gibson used a "Custom Made" plate to cover the holes that had been drilled in the top for the stop tailpiece. This guitar does, in fact, have a custom-ordered feature: the "Argentine gray" sunburst finish. Fretware/BM

▲ *Gibson ES-345TD, 1959.*
The success of the ES-335
prompted Gibson to expand
the line upward in 1959 with
two new models. In addition
to cosmetic upgrades like
double-parallelogram inlay
and gold-plated metal parts,
the ES-345 features stereo
output (which necessitates a
Y-cord) and a "Vari-tone"
rotary tone-selector switch.
The Vari-tone control did not
go over well with players.
The more expensive ES-345
sold only about a quarter as
many guitars as the ES-335.
It was discontinued in 1982.
Toby Ruckert/WC

▶ Gibson ES-355TD, 1961. The top Gibson semi-hollow model has the neck ornamentation—large block fingerboard inlay, split-diamond peghead inlay, and multiple binding—of the top model of the 1960 solidbody line, the Les Paul Custom. A vibrato is standard on the ES-355. Gruhn Guitars/DL

▼ Gibson ES-345TD, 1966. Like the ES-335, the ES-345 debuted with natural or sunburst finish, and cherry was added later in 1959. This custom color is Pelham blue. Also like the ES-335, the stop tailpiece of the ES-345 was replaced by a trapeze in 1964. Bob Christopher/DL

▲ *Gibson ES-355TD-SV, 1961. Stereo electronics and Vari-tone were offered as options on the ES-355 in 1959. Through the 1960s this optional version outsold the standard version, and the SV became standard in 1971. However, when a nonstereo, non–Vari-tone ES-355 was reintroduced in 1977, it outsold the SV. The ebony tailpiece appears on occasional examples from the early 1960s. The model was discontinued in 1982. Gruhn Guitars/WC*

◀ Gibson B. B. King Lucille, 1993. Blues artist B. B. King favored the ES-355, and he named all his guitars "Lucille." To cut down on feedback, he stuffed paper into the body through the f-holes. His Gibson endorsement models solved some of the feedback problem by eliminating the f-holes altogether. Two B. B. King models, the Standard and the Custom, debuted in 1980. In 1988 the Standard was discontinued and the Custom renamed B. B. King Lucille. The wiring is stereo with two output jacks. Gruhn Guitars/WC

▼ Gibson Trini Lopez Standard, 1966. Despite their similar names, Gibson's two Trini Lopez models have completely different bodies. The Standard is a thin semi-hollowbody with double rounded cutaways, while the Deluxe is full-depth with pointed cutaways. The ornamentation is similar on both: double-triangular fingerboard inlay, peghead with six tuners on one side, and trapeze tailpiece with wooden insert. The catalog finish on the Standard is red; this example is Pelham blue. Bob Christopher/DL

213

◀ Gibson Les Paul Signature, 1975. Gibson's original Les Paul model had a gold top finish, and, not surprisingly, the gold top was a standard finish (along with sunburst) when this hollowbody Les Paul was introduced in 1973. Early examples have oblong low-impedance pickups. From 1975 until the model's discontinuation in 1978 the pickups have both high- and low-impedance capability, accessible by a jack in the top or a second jack into the side. Dynamic Sound/BM

▼ Gibson EB-2N, 1959. A bass version of the ES-335 appeared in the spring of 1958, with a baritone tone control added in 1959. The model was discontinued in 1961 but reintroduced in 1964. Later versions included a double-pickup and a six-string bass. The EB-2 and EB-2D lasted until 1972. Clifford Antone/BM

◀ *Gibson Crest, 1969 (far left). Gibson's double-cutaway, fully hollow thinbody line consisted only of the low-end ES-330 and the Crest. The Crest's body of laminated Brazilian rosewood creates a visual sensation. The ornamental backstripe (below left) is a common feature of expensive flat-top guitars but is not found on any other Gibson archtop—electric or acoustic. Unlike any other Gibson double-cutaway electric, the back of most Crests is flat. The pickups are "floating" (not mounted into the top) like those of Gibson's most expensive endorsement model, the Johnny Smith. This is a "Gold Crest" with gold-plated parts. Silver plating was also available. Shipping records show a total of 162 Crests from 1969 to 1972. Gruhn Guitars/WC*

▶ *Gibson ES-330TD, 1966. The ES-330, introduced in 1959, appears at first glance to be a low-end version of the ES-335 with single-coil P-90 pickups instead of humbuckers. There are two fundamental differences, however. The ES-330 body is fully hollow, and the neck-body joint is at the 16th fret rather than at the 19th like the semi-hollow models. The ES-330 debuted with one or two pickups with black plastic covers; chrome-plated covers appeared in late 1962, the last year of the single-pickup model. In 1969 the ES-330 adopted the longer neck of the ES-335, but it only lasted three more years. Jacksonville Guitars/ Steve Evans*

▶ Epiphone Sheraton, 1959. The Sheraton was the only Epi hollowbody of 1958 with a model name that had not been previously used. It was also the only double-cut-away semi-hollowbody. Its fancy inlay and multiple bindings make it equivalent to Gibson's top semi-hollow model, the ES-355, but, of course, the pickups are different. Clifford Antone/BM

THINBODIES

▼ ▼ ▼

Epiphone

In 1957 Gibson's parent company bought Epiphone with the idea of acquiring Epi's acoustic bass manufacturing equipment and respected place in that market. Gibson management quickly decided, however, to take advantage of Epi's reputation as a guitar maker, and Gibson's first Epi brochure, published in 1958, pictured not only acoustic basses but also new lines of acoustic and electric guitars. The new Epiphone brand was a bit downscale from Gibson but not a budget brand. Many Gibson models had an equivalent in the Epiphone line, the main difference being that the Epis were fitted with smaller mini-humbucking pickups rather than the full-size humbuckers of high-end Gibsons.

A great deal of difference existed, however, between the Gibson-made Epis and earlier Epi models with the same names. The Emperor, Zephyr, and Century had been full-depth models prior to Gibson; in the Gibson-made line they became thinbodies.

By the mid 1960s, Epiphone models made up almost one-third of the total number of models made by Gibson, but Epiphone models from 1961 to 1970 accounted for only 14 percent of Gibson's unit sales total. Epiphone sales figures would have made a small company like Rickenbacker very happy, but they did not satisfy the Norlin company, which had bought Gibson in December 1969. In 1970 Norlin moved Epiphone production to Japan and later to Korea, and few of the subsequent models resembled the earlier American-made guitars.

◀ *Epiphone Emperor, 1961. The Emperor went from full-depth to thinbody but maintained its place at the top of the line. With a body width listed at 18 ½ inches, it is the widest standard model Gibson ever made. The Emperor retains the three pickups of the earlier Zephyr Emperor Regent. The knob placement is odd for a Gibson—almost all other f-hole models have the four knobs configured around the f-hole—but is standard for this model. The multiple laminations of the neck and the shape of the peghead indicate that the neck was part of the stockpile of parts acquired by Gibson with the purchase of Epiphone. Clifford Antone/BM*

◀ *Epiphone Century ¾, 1962. The Century had never been the lowest model in the Epi line of the 1940s and early 1950s, but it held down the bottom of the Gibson-Epi line of 1958 as the only noncutaway hollowbody electric. The full-size 16-inch model was fairly successful; this three-quarter-size, introduced in 1961, was not. It was discontinued in 1968 after a total production of only 118. Gruhn Guitars/DL*

▼ *Epiphone Zephyr, 1962. Different Epi models changed over to Gibson parts at different times. This guitar was made a year later than the Emperor (page 217), but it still has leftover Epiphone "New York" pickups and knobs while the earlier instrument has Gibson mini-humbuckers and knobs. Encore/BM*

◀ Epiphone Sheraton, 1962. Although the Sheraton was not officially offered with a cherry finish until 1965, at least one cherry run was made in 1962. Vibrato was a catalog option beginning in 1961. Production through the 1960s split almost evenly between vibrato models (308) and nonvibrato (320). Clifford Antone/BM

◀ Epiphone Riviera, 1967. An equivalent to Gibson's ES-335, the Riviera was introduced in 1962. Clifford Antone/BM

▲ *Epiphone Casino, 1961.*
The Casino, introduced in
1961, is the equivalent of the
Gibson ES-330—a fully
hollow thinbody guitar with
one or two P-90 pickups.
The dot inlay gave way to
parallelograms by 1963. The
Epiphone vibrato, featuring
a string-anchor bar of varying
diameter to compensate
for different string gauges,
was never used on a Gibson-
brand model. Gruhn Gui-
tars/DL

▶ Epiphone Caiola Custom, late 1960s. Jazz guitarist Al Caiola's endorsement model debuted in 1963. When a plainer version was added in 1966, it was named Caiola Standard and the original renamed Caiola Custom. The Custom combines deluxe ornamentation, including a Broadway-style peghead ornament, with such experimental features as a switchboard for electronics and no soundholes. Neither Caiola model was very successful. Coincidentally, the total production for both Caiola models is exactly that of the Professional—396 instruments. Pyramid/BM

◀ Epiphone Riviera 12-string, 1967. Like the ES-335, the Riviera was offered in a 12-string version beginning in 1965. Joseph Nuyens/DL

▼ *Epiphone Professional guitar and amplifier set, 1963. Gibson designers came up with the novel but seemingly workable idea of amplifier controls mounted on the guitar. The Epiphone Professional is a guitar and amp set (available with two different amps). The cord, wired permanently to the amp, connects to the guitar with a microphone-type "cannon" jack. The guitar is also wired with a standard jack so it can be used with any other amp, but the amp has no standard input. The Professional debuted in 1962 and the last set shipped in 1966 after a total of 396 guitars. Gruhn Guitars/WC*

222

◀ Rickenbacker 325, 1966. John Lennon of the Beatles played two different 325s— the short-scale, three-pickup, vibrato model. In 1984 Rickenbacker reissued his earlier modified model (he had added a Bigsby vibrato) as the 325V59 and his later 1963-style guitar as the 325V63. A third limited-edition Lennon model was offered from 1989 to 1991. Jacksonville Guitars/SE

THINBODIES

▼ ▼ ▼

Rickenbacker

Rickenbacker's original Capri or 300-series hollowbodies appeared in early 1958, and, like the solidbodies that preceded them, they were designed by Roger Rossmeisl with a unique shape that has not been copied by other makers. Only the F-series—which stands for full *width* rather than full depth—have what might be considered a conventional body shape.

In construction, too, Rickenbacker's thinbodies are unusual: hollow in a technical sense but more like solidbodies in appearance as well as performance. The top is thick, and the braces are so heavy that they almost reach the back. There is only one soundhole (none on some models), and it is usually a slash rather than a traditional *f* shape. The treble side is severely cut out to accommodate the electronics.

Another unusual characteristic of Rickenbacker's 1958 thinline hollowbody line was its model nomenclature system. It was that rarity among guitar makers, an orderly numbering system. The line comprised three model groups: short scale length with "standard" plain trim, numbered from 310 to 325; standard scale length with standard trim, 330 to 345; and standard scale with "deluxe" trim, 360 to 375. Within each of these three groups, four models were offered, and the model number increased by an increment of five for each added feature. For example, in the short scale group, model 310 had two pickups, 315 had two pickups and a vibrato, 320 had three pickups, and 325 had three pickups and a vibrato.

Originally called the Capri line, these are the models upon which Rickenbacker built its reputation as an electric guitar manufacturer, and the more popular variations still form the foundation of the Rickenbacker guitar line.

▶ *Rickenbacker 310 prototype, 1957. This early example of the short-scale, standard-trim model 310 has a longer body than the production model. The slash soundhole is unusual on a 310-series guitar. Production examples typically have no hole at all until 1961, when f-holes appear sporadically. In 1964 f-holes became standard on the short-scale models. Lloyd Chiate/BM*

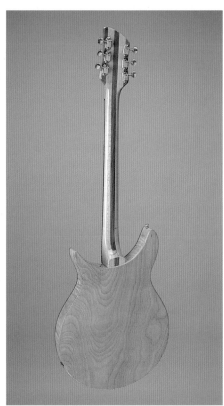

◀ *Rickenbacker 331, 1971, with Transonic amp. Inspired by nightclub light shows of the psychedelic era, Rickenbacker installed a light show in a guitar. The 331 is built around a 330 with full scale length, standard trim, two pickups, and no vibrato. The lights, which have a separate power supply, are triggered by musical tones. The 331 was made from 1970 to 1975. Scott Jennings/BM*

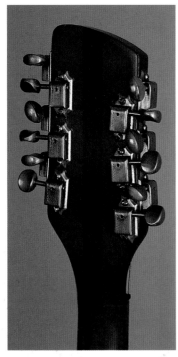

▶ *Rickenbacker 336-12, 1967. One of Rickenbacker's most successful innovations was the electric 12-string. The first one was made for George Harrison of the Beatles and was featured in his solo on "A Hard Day's Night." Roger McGuinn of the Byrds, inspired by Harrison, made the Rick 12-string the signature sound of his band. A standard 12-string version of the 330, the 330-12, was introduced in 1964. A year later this model, with a comb to convert from six- to twelve-string play, appeared. The 336-12 only lasted until 1974, but the 330-12 is still in production. Innovations include the staggered-angle tuners and reverse string configuration. On a Rick 12-string the player's down-stroke on the paired strings (tuned in octaves) hits the low string first, the opposite of accepted acoustic 12-string tuning. Gruhn Guitars/WC*

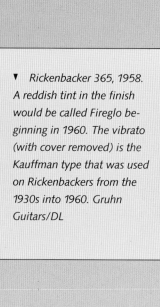

▼ *Rickenbacker 365, 1958. A reddish tint in the finish would be called Fireglo beginning in 1960. The vibrato (with cover removed) is the Kauffman type that was used on Rickenbackers from the 1930s into 1960. Gruhn Guitars/DL*

▲ *Rickenbacker 360, 1958. Rickenbacker's deluxe package consisted of body binding and large wedge-shaped fingerboard inlay. This early example sports what would come to be known as Autumnglo finish. Like the 330, the 360 was offered successfully as a 12-string and not so successfully with the 6–12 converter comb. Gil Southworth/BM*

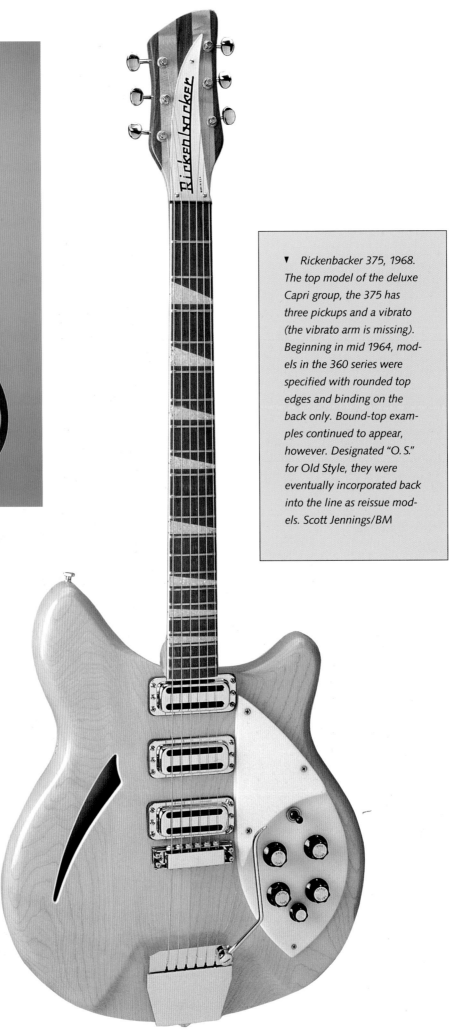

▼ *Rickenbacker 375, 1968. The top model of the deluxe Capri group, the 375 has three pickups and a vibrato (the vibrato arm is missing). Beginning in mid 1964, models in the 360 series were specified with rounded top edges and binding on the back only. Bound-top examples continued to appear, however. Designated "O. S." for Old Style, they were eventually incorporated back into the line as reissue models. Scott Jennings/BM*

▶ *Rickenbacker 4005-8, 1968. In the footsteps of Rick's 12-string guitar, a bass equivalent appeared in the late 1960s. The eight strings are arranged in pairs and tuned in octaves. Scott Jennings/BM*

◀ *Rickenbacker 4005WB, late 1960s. When the 4005, Rickenbacker's Capri-style bass, was introduced in 1965, Capri models had the rounded, unbound top border. In 1966 a bound-top, old-style variation was added and dubbed 4005WB (for White Binding). The black finish is Jetglo. Jay Haskett/BM*

▼ *Rickenbacker 330F, 1958. The F-series models debuted shortly after the Capris. Although the Fs are entirely different in body shape and depth—2½ inches compared with 1½—they follow the same pattern for hardware and ornamentation. Like the 330, the 330F has two pickups, no vibrato, and standard trim. (The short-scale 310–325 style was not available in the F-series.) Natural finish eventually became known in the Rickenbacker lexicon of "glo" finishes as Mapleglo. Scott Jennings/BM*

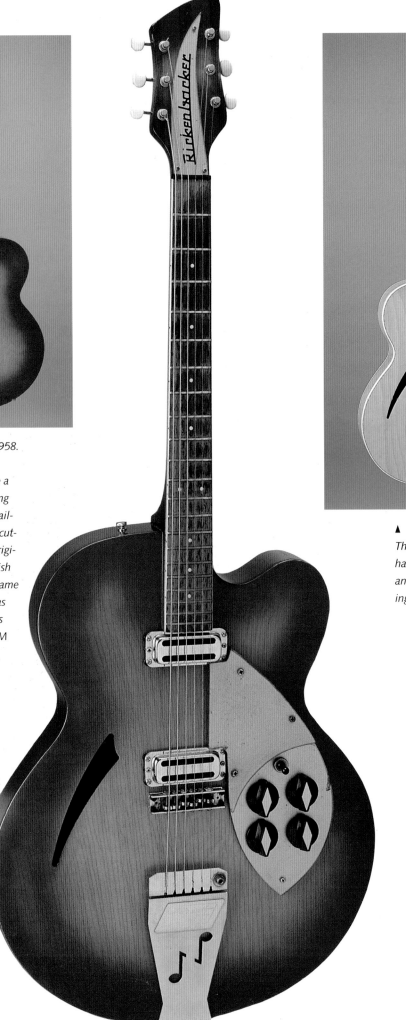

▶ *Rickenbacker 335F, 1958. All Capris with a model number ending in 5 have a vibrato. The arm is missing from this example. The tailpiece with musical-note cutouts is uncommon but original. The red sunburst finish (above) had no official name at the time this guitar was made, but by 1960 it was Fireglo. Eugene Fields/BM*

▲ *Rickenbacker 375F, 1960. The top model of the F-series has three pickups, a vibrato, and deluxe inlay and binding. Silver Strings/BM*

▼ Rickenbacker 360F prototype, 1961. The carved "lip" around the top is found on many German guitars, and German-born designer Roger Rossmeisl brought it to the United States. This is one of two 360F prototypes with the special top carving. Real Guitars/BM

▶ *Old Kraftsman, mid 1950s. Old Kraftsman instruments were made by Kay, and in the Kay line this is a K-161, the Thin Twin. Kay responded to Fender and Gibson solidbodies in 1953 with this unusual thick flat top. It is commonly known as the Jimmy Reed model, after the blues artist. Nutty Jazz Guitars/BM*

THINBODIES

▼ ▼ ▼

Other Makers

By the 1960s the majority of electric guitarists no longer demanded any significant acoustic qualities from their instruments, but the aesthetic appeal of a hollowbody design still mattered. Consequently, the most popular hollowbody or semi-hollow guitars had the appearance of hollowbody construction—typically with a standard body shape and soundholes in the top—but with a body depth thinner than the standard three inches of an acoustic archtop. Many Gretsch models evolved gradually to a thinbody depth, and those, as well as a few later models that were always thinbodies, are discussed with Gretsch full-depth archtops.

▲ Kay Jazz II, 1961, with Fender Bassman amp, 1959. Kay modeled this thinbody double-cutaway after Gibson's ES-335. Blues-rock guitar legend Eric Clapton played this model in his early years. Danny Davenport and Joey Davenport/Danny Davenport

▲ Harmony Rocket III, mid-1960s, with Supro Statesman amplifier, 1967. Harmony gave Kay heavy competition in the budget market. The Meteor led Harmony's thin-bodies in 1958. The Rockets followed in 1960, and the Rocket III was the most expensive, with a list price of $139.50. The Supro ampli-fier, with two 12-inch Jensen speakers, listed for $450. Danny Davenport (guitar), Travis Tritt (amp)/Danny Davenport

◄ Kay Barney Kessel Pro, late 1950s. Jazz guitarist Barney Kessel endorsed a line of Kay models in 1957 before moving to Gibson in 1961. The Pro appeared in 1954 as Kay's answer to Gib-son's Les Paul and subse-quently became the third and smallest model in the Kay Kessel line. Charley's/BM

▼ *Martin F-55, 1962. Martin attacked the electric guitar market in 1961 with the single-pickup F-50, the double-pickup F-55, and the double-cutaway, double-pickup F-65. The DeArmond pickups are similar to those used by Gretsch until 1958, but they were outdated by the time Martin electrics appeared. Martin's foray made only a small dent in the market—total electric production of electric F models and the two G models that replaced them was 2,860 from 1961 to 1967. Gruhn Guitars/DL*

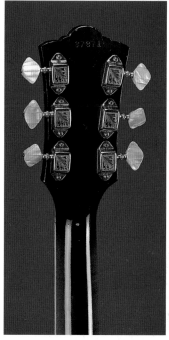

◀ *Guild DE-500, 1964. Duane Eddy's "twangy" guitar sound, which he got from a Gretsch Chet Atkins Hollow Body, made him the most popular solo guitarist of the late 1950s. In 1961 he sought his own endorsement deal, and Guild was the first company to show interest. The Duane Eddy model was based on Guild's T-500, a limited-run thinbody version of the Stuart 500 archtop. Eddy specified two features from his Gretsch: Bigsby vibrato and master volume control on the cutaway bout. Examples from 1962 and 1963 have single-coil DeArmond pickups; mini-humbucking pickups appeared in 1964. The DE-500 was last made in 1969 but was reissued in 1983. Pyramid Guitars/BM*

▼ Guild DE-400, 1966. In 1963 Guild introduced this cheaper version of the DE-500. All the differences are cosmetic, including chrome-plated metal parts, a different peghead logo, and less binding. As is usually the case, the cheaper model was the more successful. Estimated production totals, beginning in 1965, are 201 for the DE-400 (which was last made in 1968) and 41 for the DE-500. Gruhn Guitars/DL

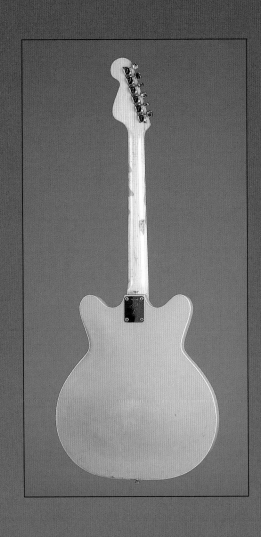

▶ *Fender Coronado II, circa 1968. Under CBS's ownership Fender expanded its model line considerably in the late 1960s. Former Rickenbacker designer Roger Rossmeisl had joined Fender in 1962 to develop an acoustic line, and in 1966 he brought forth a new thinline electric. Coronados were available in custom colors, such as this sonic blue, and with one pickup (Coronado I), two pickups, or two pickups with vibrato. Gruhn Guitars/DL*

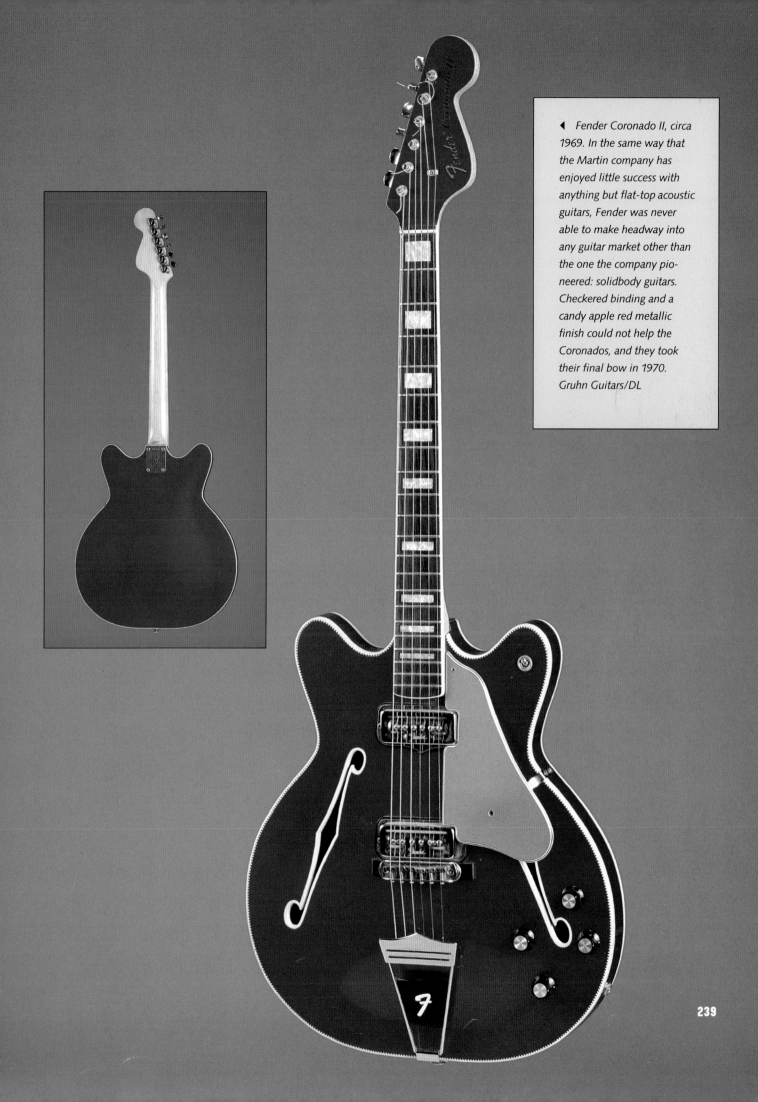

◀ Fender Coronado II, circa 1969. In the same way that the Martin company has enjoyed little success with anything but flat-top acoustic guitars, Fender was never able to make headway into any guitar market other than the one the company pioneered: solidbody guitars. Checkered binding and a candy apple red metallic finish could not help the Coronados, and they took their final bow in 1970. Gruhn Guitars/DL

▲ Fender Coronado II, Wildwood III, circa 1967. Wildwood coloration was unpredictable and inconsistent, but Fender did its best to group the wood into six colors. Wildwood III denotes orange. Walter Carter/WC

▶ Fender Coronado II, Wildwood II, circa 1967. "Wildwood" was the patented product of a Scandinavian chemist who injected a solution into beechwood trees that caused the wood to change color. Fender acquired exclusive rights to Wildwood and in 1966 introduced it on two models: a Kingman-style (dreadnought) flat top and the Coronado II. Wildwood II was the designation for this greenish hue. Gruhn Guitars/DL

▶ *Fender Coronado II Bass, 1967. Like the Coronado guitars, the Coronado Bass was offered with one or two pickups. Jacksonville Guitars/SE*

▼ *Fender Coronado XII, circa 1966. The Coronado line included a 12-string from 1966 through 1969. Gruhn Guitars/WC*

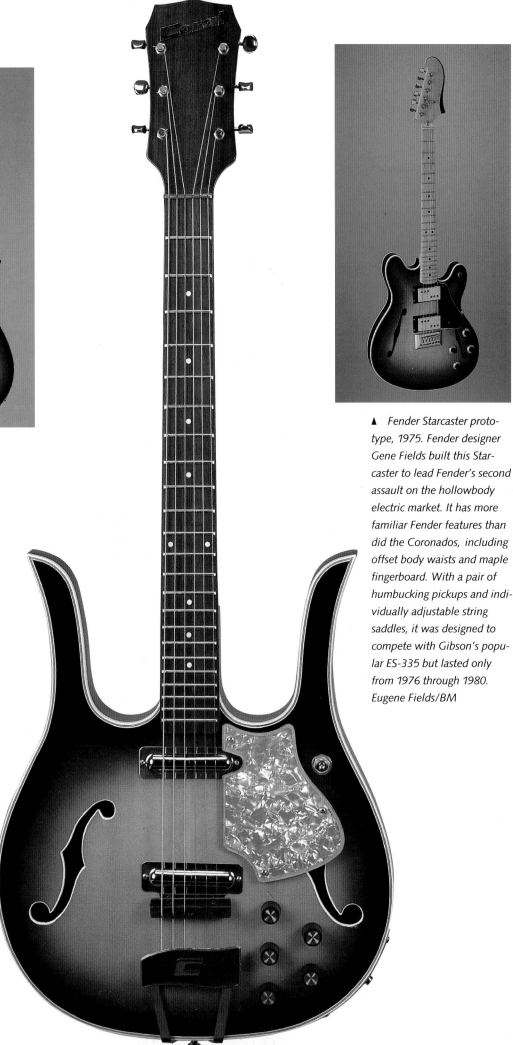

▼ *Coral Longhorn, 1968. Danelectro, the company famous for building Sears, Roebuck's Silvertone amp-in-case models in the mid 1960s, introduced this body shape with an extra-long 31-fret neck in 1958 on a model called the Guitarlin and a companion bass called the Longhorn. M.C.A. bought Danelectro in late 1967 and introduced the Coral brand so that Danelectro could have its own line to compete with its Sears products. The Coral version of the Guitarlin, called simply the Longhorn, has the lipstick-tube pickups that have practically become a Danelectro trademark. By the end of 1968 M.C.A. had shut down Danelectro. George Bradfute/DL*

▲ *Fender Starcaster prototype, 1975. Fender designer Gene Fields built this Starcaster to lead Fender's second assault on the hollowbody electric market. It has more familiar Fender features than did the Coronados, including offset body waists and maple fingerboard. With a pair of humbucking pickups and individually adjustable string saddles, it was designed to compete with Gibson's popular ES-335 but lasted only from 1976 through 1980. Eugene Fields/BM*

◄ *Micro-Frets Golden Melody, circa 1972. Micro-Frets of Frederick, Maryland, took its name from the adjustable nut and stayed in business from 1965 to 1972. The Golden Melody model held a place in the lower to middle level of the line. Gruhn Guitars/WC*

The Future of the Guitar

As the twentieth century nears its end, the future of the guitar remains open for debate. Practically all the major innovations in guitar design were accomplished by the time this century was barely half over, hardly an encouraging fact. The various acoustic guitar styles—flat top, archtop, and resonator—had all reached their zenith by the mid 1930s, and the same forces that drove their evolution drove the development of the electric guitar in the 1930s. Setting aside the manufacturing hiatus caused by World War II, the evolution of the electric guitar from Adolph Rickenbacker's Frying Pan to Leo Fender's Telecaster was completed in less than 15 years.

To the largest segment of the American population—the postwar baby boomers—the 1950s may seem like yesterday, but the fact is that the 1950s happened a *long* time ago. In the 1990s, when the flood of technological advances can make new TVs, computers, or even electronic keyboard instruments obsolete every few months, 40 years is an eternity.

There have been innovations in guitar design since the 1950s, to be sure, but they have been refinements rather than revolutions. Pickups have been developed that give a truer sound to an amplified acoustic guitar, an innovation that has freed flat-top body designs to some extent. Vibratos have been improved so that electric guitarists can achieve "dive bomb" effects without going out of tune. The market for "outboard" gear and effects—the equipment that processes the signal coming from an electric guitar—has grown, but the guitar that creates the signal is still the basic six-string electric.

Modern materials have had only a limited impact. National's fiberglass map-shaped electrics failed; the fiberglass shell backs of Ovation's flat-top guitars gained respectable commercial success, helped along by the company's pioneering position in the electrified flat-top market. Carbon-graphite necks and bodies have proven suitable for guitars but have not seriously threatened traditional wood construction.

Variations on the standard six-string guitar have found limited acceptance. Only a handful of players are closely identified with 12-string models, fewer with seven-string guitars. The twangy sound of a low-tuned guitar, known as a six-string bass or baritone guitar, goes in and out of fashion, but no well-known artist plays a six-string baritone guitar exclusively. The electric sitar is viewed as a gimmick.

The electronic age has given rise to two new instruments that are more than specialty guitars. One is the synthesizer guitar, a hybrid product of the keyboard revolution of the 1980s. In concept, it is simply a guitar driving a synthesizer rather than a magnetic pickup. The synthesizer needs information on which of the six strings is being played (right-hand action) and where on the fingerboard those strings are being fretted (left-hand action), but the two areas of the guitar do not have to be connected, although a guitarist would feel more at home playing a synthesizer guitar built along the lines of a standard guitar. This instrument would seem to be a shortcut, a synthesizer made for guitarists who do not know how to play a keyboard, much as the tenor banjo was thought to be a banjo for mandolin players who could not play banjo—until the tenor overshadowed both the five-string banjo and the mandolin. However, despite a promising start in the 1980s, neither the synthesizer guitar nor the keyboard synthesizer have been able to unseat the guitar as the most popular mass-market instrument.

Unlike the guitar synthesizer, which still plays like a guitar, the Chapman Stick is unique among descendants of the guitar. The playing technique for guitar and all other fretted instruments does not carry over to the Stick. It was designed to exploit fretboard tapping techniques that were developed on a standard guitar primarily by Gretsch employee Jimmie Webster. Although the stick has the appearance of a guitar—with strings, frets, and a pickup unit—all the fingers of both hands are free to produce tones. Since it is an entirely new instrument, it offers no easier transition to a guitarist than a piano would, and consequently it has attracted only a small following.

The future of electric guitars—at least the near future of the market for new electric guitars—may well be in the past. One trend of the early 1990s is greater appreciation for older, traditional designs. Many companies, including Fender, Gibson, Rickenbacker, and a revived Gretsch, have found a strong market for vintage reissues.

The increasing popularity of both vintage reissues and original vintage guitars suggests that the electric guitar reached its evolutionary peak several

◀ *Chapman Stick, 1993. The Stick is the most radical and practical innovation to appear in the stringed instrument world in centuries. Emmett Chapman of southern California, a former guitarist, built his first Stick in 1969. It was designed strictly for tapping the strings against the fingerboard (rather than fretting with one hand and picking with the other), but, more importantly, it gave the finger-tapper full use of all ten fingers, resulting in a much wider range of harmonic and rhythmic possibilities than that available to a guitarist. Stick Enterprises, founded in 1974, reports cumulative sales of "several thousand" Sticks. Sticks are available in a variety of hardwoods; this example is teak. Stick Enterprises*

decades ago. This is not necessarily cause for alarm among guitar lovers, however. Considering that acoustic flat-top design was well-evolved by the 1850s and violin design hit its peak 300 years ago, the electric guitar as we know it today should be around for a long time to come.

BIBLIOGRAPHY
▼ ▼ ▼

Bacon, Tony and Paul Day. *The Fender Book*. San Francisco: GPI/Miller Freeman Books, 1992.

____. *The Les Paul Book*. San Francisco: GPI/Miller Freeman Books, 1993.

Brozman, Bob. *The History & Artistry of National Resonator Instruments*. Fullerton, Calif.: Centerstream Publishing, 1993.

Duchossoir, A. R. *The Fender Stratocaster*. Rev. ed. Milwaukee: Hal Leonard Publishing Corporation, 1990.

___. *Gibson Electrics, Vol. 1*. Milwaukee: Hal Leonard Publishing Corporation, 1981.

___. *Guitar Identification*. 3d ed. Milwaukee: Hal Leonard Publishing Corporation, 1990.

___. *The Fender Telecaster*. Milwaukee: Hal Leonard Publishing Corporation, 1991.

Gruhn, George, and Walter Carter. *Gruhn's Guide to Vintage Guitars*. San Francisco: GPI/Miller Freeman Books, 1991.

Longworth, Mike. *Martin Guitars: A History*. 3d ed. Nazareth, Penn.: Mike Longworth, 1988.

Read, Oliver, and Walter L. Welch. *From Tin Foil to Stereo: Evolution of the Phonograph*, 2d ed. Indianapolis: Howard W. Sams and Co., Inc., 1976.

Schmidt, Paul William. *Acquired of the Angels: The Lives and Works of Master Guitar Makers John D'Angelico and James D'Aquisto*. Metuchen, NJ: The Scarecrow Press, Inc., 1991

Scott, Jay. *'50s Cool: Kay Guitars*. New York: Seventh String Press, 1992.

____. *The Guitars of the Fred Gretsch Company*. Fullerton, Calif.: Centerstream Publishing, 1992.

Smith, Richard. *The Complete History of Rickenbacker Guitars*. Fullerton, Calif.: Centerstream Publishing, 1987.

Wheeler, Tom. *American Guitars: An Illustrated History*. New York: HarperCollins, 1990.

White, Forrest. *Fender: The Inside Story*. San Francisco: GPI/Miller Freeman Books, 1994.

INDEX

▼ ▼ ▼

▼ References to photo-
graphs are printed in *italics*.

Alembic bass, *200*
Alkire E-Harp, 24, *38*
Alkire, Eddie, 38
Aluminum Alloy Casting
    Co., 10
Ampeg, 133
    Baby Bass, *114*
    Dan Armstrong, *199*
    f-hole guitar, *198*
App, *52*
Appleton, O.W., 52
Armstrong, Dan, 199
Atkins, Chet, 170, 180

Bajo sexto, 134
Baldwin, 91
Bar-Rashi, 199
Barnes & Reinecke, 29
Beatles, 192, 225, 226
Beauchamp, George, 9,
    10, 14, 15
Bell, Vincent, 192
Berry, Chuck, 205
Bigsby guitar, *52*
Bigsby, Paul, 52, 116
Birdland, 204
Bohannon, Gary, 3
Bronson lap steel, *19*
Buttleman, C.V., 44
Byrd, Billy, 204
Byrd, Jerry, 10
Byrds, 226

Caiola, Al, 221
Carson, Bill, 125
Carter, Walter, 3
CBS Records, 117, 238
Century Singing Electric,
    10
Chapman Stick, *244*, 245
Chapman, Emmett, 244
Christian, Charlie, 55, 56,
    58
Clapton, Eric, 233
CLF Research, 117
CMI, 83, 109, 193

Collins Kids, Larry and
    Lorrie, 196
Conn, C. G, 83
Cooder, Ry, 18
Coppock Deluxe, *iv*, *18*
Coral
    Electric sitar, 2, 114,
        192
    Guitarlin, *242*
    Longhorn, *242*
Crescendo, 6, 44, 45

D'Angelico, 77
Danelectro, 38, 114, 172,
    193
    Bass, *191*
    Doubleneck, *191*
    Guitarlin, 190
    Longhorn 6-string
    bass, *190*
    Sitar, *192*
    U-2, *190*
Daniel, Nathan (Nat),
    190, 191, 192
DeArmond, 86, 90, 234,
    235, 242
Diddley, Bo, 201, 202
Dixon, Dean, 3
Dobro, 7, 14, 15
    All Electric, *48*
    Electric Hawaiian, *14*
    Spanish-neck electric,
        15
Dopyera brothers, 15
Dopyera, John, 14
Douglas, Jerry, 18
Dronge, Alfred, 110
Duco colors, 140, 142
DuPont, 140, 142, 144

Eddy, Duane, 235
Edwards, Nokie, 195
Electar, 35
Electro, 10
Emmons, Buddy, 41
Epiphone, 1, 3, 7, 21, 51,
    64, 107, 110, 112,
    158, 216–222
    Alkire E-Harp, *38*

Epiphone *(continued)*
    Broadway, 83, *87*, 221
    Broadway custom, *87*
    Caiola Custom, *221*
    Casino, *220*
    Century, 87, 217, 218
    Century ¾, *218*
    Coronet, *193*
    Crestwood Deluxe, *193*
    De Luxe, 82
    Electrophone, *37*
    Emperor, 82, *85*, 87,
        110, *217*, 218
    M, *35*
    Professional, 221, *222*
    Riviera, *219*
    Riviera 12-string, *221*
    Roberts, Howard, 83,
        88
    Sheraton, 87, *216*, *219*
    Varichord, *36*
    Volpe, Harry, *86*
    Zephyr, *59*, 82, *86*,
        87, *217*, *218*
    Zephyr Cutaway, *86*
    Zephyr De Luxe, *82*
    Zephyr De Luxe
        Regent, *83*, *84*
    Zephyr Emperor
        Regent, *85*, 217
Evans, Steve, 3

Farlow, Tal, 78
Fender, 3, 32, 31–34, 64,
    46, 66, 107,
    115–147, 148,
    149, 168, 171,
    172, 181, 191,
    232, 246
    Arrow, *131*
    Bass protoype, *138*
    Bass V, *138*
    Bass VI, *137i*, 138
    Bassman amp, *124*,
        233
    Broadcaster, 116, *121*,
    122
    Champ, 31
    Champion, *31*, 32

Fender *(continued)*
    Coronado, 125, 134,
        238, *239*, *240*
    Coronado Bass, *241*
    Coronado XII, *241*
    Custom, 131
    Custom color chart,
        142, 143
    Custom Telecaster,
        126, 142
    Deluxe, 32, *33*
    Dual 6 Professional,
        34
    Dual 8 Professional, *34*
    Duo-Sonic, 125, *130*,
        146
    Electric XII, *131*, 138
    Esquire, 49, *115*, 116,
        121, *124*, 125,
        133, 139, *145*, 146
    Esquire Custom 125
    Esquire prototype, *120*
    Guitar prototype,
        1943, *119–120*
    Jaguar, 124, 125, *131*,
        144
    Jazz bass 134, *136*,
        137, 138, *145*,
        146, 157
    Jazzmaster, 124, 125,
        130, 131, 137,
        141, *146*
    Kingman, 240
    LTD, *113*
    Mandolin, *132*
    Mary Kaye, *140*
    Maverick, 131
    Model 26 amp, 32, *33*
    Musiclander, *131*
    Musicmaster, 125,
        130, 131, 146
    Mustang, 131
    No-caster, *122*
    Organ Button, 32, *33*
    Precision, 34, 114,
        117, 124, *133*,
        134, *135*, 138,
        139, *143*, 157
    Princeton, 32, *33*

Fender *(continued)*
    Princeton amp, 32, *33*
    Professional amp, 32,
        33
    Squier, 117
    Starcaster, *242*
    Stratocaster, 2, 3, 34,
        117, 124, 125,
        127, *128*, *129*,
        130, 131, 132,
        139, *140*, 141,
        142, *143*, *144*,
        145, 182, 195
    Stringmaster, *34*
    Student, 32, *33*
    Swinger, *131*
    Telecaster, 32, 34,
        116, 117, *122*,
        123, 125, 126,
        127, 131, 132,
        134, 135, 139,
        141, *145*, *146*,
        147, 149, 157,
        182, 193, 245
    Telecaster Bass, *138*,
        147
    Telecaster Custom,
        125
    Telecaster prototype,
        126
    Telecaster Thinline,
        125, *126*
    Telecaster Wildwood
        Thinline, *125*
    Vibroverb amp, *129*
    Violin, *132*
    Wildwood, 125, 240
Fender, Leo, 3, 31, 32, 52,
    115, 116, 117,
    201, 245
Fender Sales, 181
Fields, Gene, 242
Fullerton, George, 117,
    141

G&L, 117
    Broadcaster, *201*
Garland, Hank, 204
Gentry, Robert, 197

Gibson, 1, 3, 6, 7, 20–30, 31, 38, 41, 42, 44, 52, 61, 64, 65–81, 82, 83, 87, 107, 109, 112, 116, 126, 133, 148–170, 193, 203–215, 216, 217, 218, 219, 220, 232, 246
25th Anniversary Les Paul, 159
Atkins, Chet, CE, 170
Atkins, Chet, SST, 170
Black Beauty, 152
Byrdland, 204, 205
Century-10, 38
CF-100E, 81
Consolette, 30
Country Gentleman, 98
Crest, 215
Custom color chart, 168
Doubleneck Hawaiian, 25
EA-400 amp, 74
EB, 157
EB-0, 157
EB-1, 157
EB-2, 157, 214
EB-3, 157
EBS-1250, 166
EDS-1275, 165
EH-100, 22, 24
EH-125, 24
EH-150, 22, 23, 25
EH-150 13-string, 24
EH-150 Hackman, 23
EH-185, 26
EH-630, 28
Electraharp, 27, 28, 36
EMS-1235, 165
EPB, 58
ERB, 58
ES-5, 66, 68, 69, 73, 116
ES-5 Switchmaster, 69
ES-100, 56
ES-125, -125T, 125TC, 56, 65, 65, 66, 67, 80, 207
ES-135, 67
ES-140, -140T, 71, 206
ES-150, 55, 56, 65, 66, 67
ES-150DC, 80
ES-175, 70, 71, 72, 80, 87, 109, 203
ES-175CC, 55
ES-225, 203, 204
ES-250, 55, 56

Gibson (continued)
ES-295, 71, 203
ES-300, 57, 58, 65, 67
ES-330, 215, 220
ES-335, v, 2, 80, 204, 208, 211, 216, 219, 221, 242
ES-335-12, 209
ES-335DOT, 208
ES-345, 210
ES-350, 66, 67
ES-350/ES-5, 66
ES-350T, 205
ES-355, 211, 212
ES-775, 72
ETB, 58
Explorer, 3, 30, 149, 162, 163, 164
F-5, 3, 42
Farlow, Tal, 78, 79
Firebirds, 79, 149, 166, 167, 168, 169
Flying V, 3, 30, 149, 162, 164
Fretless Wonder, 152
Futura, 160
J-160E, 81
J-200, 78
Kessel, Barney, 77
King, B. B., 213
L-5, 2, 68, 73
L-5, 170
L-5C, 206
L-5CES, 72, 73
L-5CES, 204
L-5CT, 206
L-5S, 170
L-6S Deluxe, 170
L-6S, 170
L-7ED, 68
Les Paul (Model and Standard), 2, 3, 30, 52, 71, 116, 148, 149, 150, 151, 152, 154, 157, 158, 162, 166, 170, 171, 172, 182, 203, 214, 233
Les Paul 25th Anniversary, 159
Les Paul Artisan, 159
Les Paul Classic, 158
Les Paul Custom, 150, 152, 152, 154, 156, 158, 159, 166
Les Paul Custom, 211
Les Paul Deluxe, 158
Les Paul Junior, 152, 153, 154, 157, 166
Les Paul Junior, 152, 156
Les Paul Recording, 158

Gibson (continued)
Les Paul/SG Custom Tenor, 156
Les Paul/SG Custom, 155
Les Paul/SG Standard, 155, 156
Les Paul Signature, 214
Les Paul Special, 154, 155, 166
Les Paul Studio Lite, 158
Les Paul Studio, 158
Les Paul TV ¾, 153, 154
Les Paul, The, 160–161, 162
Lopez, Trini, 79, 213
Lucille, 213
Melody Maker, 149
Metalbody steel, 20, 21
Moderne, 164
Paul, Les, see Les Paul
SG Special, 154
SGs, 149, 155, 157, 166
Skylark, 30
Smith, Johnny, 77, 88
Style 5, 42
Super 300CES, 76
Super 400C, 73
Super 400CES, 1, 73, 74, 76, 204
Super 400CES custom, 75
Tennessean, 98
The Les Paul, 160–161, 162
Thunderbirds, 166, 169
Ultratone, 29, 20
Violins, 83
Gibson, Orville, 3
Gittler, 199
Gittler, Alan, 199
Gobel, George, 206
Godfrey, Arthur, 173
Gretsch, 17, 64, 86, 89–106, 107, 117, 122, 140, 170, 171–185, 201, 234, 246
Anniversary, 104, 105
Atkins Axe, 180
Atkins, Chet, Country Gentleman, 97, 98, 170
Atkins, Chet, Hollow Body, 90, 95, 96, 175, 140, 235
Atkins, Chet, Nashville, 97
Atkins, Chet, Solid Body, i, 90, 174, 175

Gretsch (continued)
Atkins, Chet, Tennessean, 97, 98
Atkins Super Axe, 180
Bikini, 178
Broadkaster, 122
Champagne Sparkle Jet, 179
Convertible, 103
Corvette, 90, 94, 179
Corvette Gold Duke, 179
Country Club, 90, 92, 93, 101, 104, 140
Custom 6 117, 105
Duo-Jet Tenor, 173
Duo-Jet, 171, 172, 173, 174, 179
Electro II 6192-3, 89, 90, 91
Electromatic Spanish, 90
Electromatic steel, 37, 38
Electromatic Twin amp, 102
Gold Duke, 179
Goody, Sam, 106
Hi-Roller, 180
Jet Airliner, 17
Jet Firebird, 173
Monkees, 106
Nashville, 97
Round-Up, 174
Salvador, Sal, 104
Silver Jet, 171
Southern Belle, 98
Streamliner, 90, 94
Streamliner Special, 95
Synchromatic, 90, 103
Tennessean, 97, 98
Viking, 106
White Falcon, 93, 100–101, 102, 103, 140, 176
White Penguin, 176–177
Gretsch, Fred, 91
Guild, 107
A-500, 111
DE-400, 236–237
DE-500, 235, 237
Polara S-100, 194
Stratford 375, 110
Stuart 500, 111
T-500, 235
X-350, 110
X-375, 110
X-550, 112
Guitarron, 134

Hackman, Chuck, 23

Hall, F.C., 10, 181
Harlin Brothers, 27, 37
Multi-Kord, 41
Harmony, 10, 38
Rocket III, 234
Meteor, 234
Harp guitar, 2
Harrison, George, 192, 226
Hart, Guy, 21
Holly, Buddy, 39
Holmes Bo Diddley Cadillac, 201
Holmes, Tom, 201
Hull, Everett, 114, 133, 134
Hyatt, Dale, 117

Isaacs, Bud, 36

Jackson, Shot, 41

K&F, 32, 116, 120
Steels, 33
Kalamazoo Gazette, 27
Kauffman, Doc, 31, 32, 50, 55
Kay, 7, 232, 234
Jazz II, 233
K-161, 232
Kessell, Barney, Pro, 233
Thin Twin, 232
Kay, John, 107
Kaye, Mary, 140
Kessell, Barney, 77, 79, 233

Larson Brothers, 51
Lennon, John, 81, 223
Lindley, David, 11
Loar, Lloyd, 21, 42–46, 133
Loftin, Dan, 3
Log, 51, 116
Lopez, Trini, 79
Lucas, Nick, 149
Ludwig drums, 199

Maganatone headless steel, 39, 202
Magna Electronics, 39
Manny's, 105
Maphis, Joe, 196
Marker, Wilbur, 27
Martin, 7, 21, 64, 107, 239
00-18E, 113
D-18E, 113
D-28E, 113
D-45, 2
Dreadnought, 2, 21
F-55, 234

Martin, C. F., 3
Matses, 36
MCA, 242
McCarty, Ted, 68, 83,
    148, 206
McGuinn, Roger, 226
Meissner Inventions, 59
Melobar Powerslide, 40
Micro-Frets Golden
    Melody, 243
Micro-Frets Husky bass,
    200
Mitchell, Billy, 3
Montgomery Ward, 25
Moore, John, 27
Morrel, 36
Moseley, Semie, 195, 196,
    197
Moser, Neil, 202
Mosrite
    Custom, 197
    Doubleneck, 196
    Joe Maphis, 196
    Ventures, 195, 196
Multi-Kord, 27, 37, 41
Music Man, 117

NAMM, 116
National, 1, 3, 7, 9,
    14–19, 55, 64, 107
    Bel-Aire, 109
    Club Combo, 108
    Console, 16
    Debonaire custom, 108
    Duolian, 15
    Dynamic, 17, 18
    Electric Hawaiian, 14
    Electric Spanish, 5, 53
    Glenwood 95, 187
    Glenwood, 186
    Grand Console, 16
    Map-shapes, 15
    New Yorker, 16, 18
    New Yorker Spanish,
        53, 54
    Newport 82, 187
    Newport 84, 187
    Newport 88, 188
    Pedal steel, 17
    Rocket 110, 17
    Silvo, 15, 54
    Studio 66, 189
    Style O, 15, 18, 54
    Tri-Plex Chord
        Changer, 17
    Triolian, 15
    Val-Pro, 187
    Westwood 72, 188,
        189
    Westwood 75, 188
    Westwood 77, 188
Newton, Mike, 3
Nighthawk, Robert, 179

Norlin, 217
Northwestern University,
    46

Old Kraftsman, 232
Original Musical Instru-
    ment Co., 15
Ovation, 245

Paul, Les, 51, 66, 116, 148,
    149, 158, 159, 202
Paul, Les, The Log, 51, 116
Pierce, Webb 36
Premier Aquarium, 39

Radio-Tel, 10, 181, 182
Rajah Zeetar, 118
Randall, 117
Recording King Roy
    Smeck, 25
Rey, Alvino, 27
Rickenbacker 8–13, 35, 37,
    38, 133, 134,
    181–185, 217,
    223–231, 238, 246
    59 lap steel, 13
    100 lap steel, 13
    300-series, 223, 224
    310 prototype, 224
    325 guitar, 223
    330 guitar, 225, 226,
        228
    330-12 guitar, 226
    330F, 229
    331 Light Show, 225
    335F, 230
    336-12 guitar, 226
    360 guitar, 228
    360F prototype, 231
    365 guitar, 227
    375 guitar, 228
    375F, 230
    381 guitar, 107
    4000 bass, 182, 184, 185
    4001 bass, 184
    4005-8 bass, 229
    A-22, 11
    A-25, 8, 9
    Amplifier, 11, 13
    B (Bakelite), 12, 48, 115
    Combo 425, 184
    Combo 450, 183, 184,
        185
    Combo 450-12, 184
    Combo 460, 184
    Combo 600, 181, 182
    Combo 800, 181, 182,
        183
    DC-16, 12, 13
    Electro Mandolin, 60
    Electro Spanish, 48
    Electro Tenor, 60
    F-series, 223

Rickenbacker (continued)
    Frying Pan, 8, 9, 10, 11,
        12, 14, 15, 20, 47,
        245
    G, 13
    Lap steels, 11
    Mandolin, 11, 60, 185
    NS, 13
    Silver Hawaiian, 13
    SP, 107
    Spanish neck archtop,
        10, 13
    Tenor guitar, 11
    Vibrola Spanish, 50
Rickenbacker, Adolph, 3,
    9, 10, 14, 15, 18,
    19, 21, 31, 45,
    181, 245
Rickenbacker, Eddie, 9
Rico, Bernard C., 202
Ro-Pat-In, 7, 9, 10, 45
Roberts, Howard, 88
Rossmeisl, Roger, 113,
    223, 231, 238

Sears, Roebuck, 38, 190,
    193, 242
Sho-Bud, 41
Silvertone, 190, 242
    Guitar/Amp combo,
        193
    Steel, 38
Siminoff, Roger, 3
Slingerland Songster, 49,
    115–116
Smeck Roy, 25, 149
Smith, Johnny, 77, 111
Smith, Ted, 40
Smith, Walter, 40
Sprung, John, 3
Stathopoulo family, 82, 83
Steinberger, 39
    Bass, 202
Steinberger, Ned, 202
Steppenwolf, 107
Stick, 244
Stromberg-Voisinet, 6, 7,
    44
Sunshine, Herb, 59
Supro, 14, 15
    Clipper, 31
    Electric Hawaiian, 14
    Lap steel, 18
    Statesman amp, 234
Synthesizer guitar, 246

Travis, Merle, 52, 75

Valco, 14, 15, 18, 19, 37,
    38, 64, 108
Vega, 6, 7, 44
    Six-string tenor, 198
    Tenor guitar, 61

Vivi-Tone, 3, 21, 42,
    44–46
    Acousti, 46
    Clavier, 45
    Electric Spanish, 42, 43
    Mandolin, 46
    Mandocello, 46
Volpe, Harry, 86

Walker, Tom, 117
Webster, Jimmie, 90, 246
White, Forrest, 117
Williams, L. A., 44
Wurlitzer, 46